D1489520

MAY

Make the Most of Every Month with Carson-Dellosa's Monthly Books!

Production Manager
Chris McIntyre

Editorial Director
Jennifer Weaver-Spencer

Writers
Lynette Pyne
Amy Gamble
Karen M. Smith

Editors
Carol Layton
Kelly Gunzenhauser
Maria McKinney
Hank Rudisill

Art Directors
Penny Casto
Alain Barsony

Illustrators
Courtney Bunn
Mike Duggins
Edward Fields
Erik Huffine
David Lackey
Ray Lambert
Bill Neville
Betsy Peninger
J.J. Rudisill
Pam Thayer
Julie Webb

Cover Design
Amber Kocher Crouch
Ray Lambert
J.J. Rudisill

Flower Seeds

Carson-Dellosa Publishing Company, Inc.

MAY

Table of Contents

MAY TEACHER TIPS

Read All About It
Tantalize students into reading about upcoming themes in the classroom. Gather a box of books on subjects that students will be studying soon and place them in the reading center. Then, post a sign on the box that says, "DO NOT READ THESE BOOKS!" After a week, students will be thrilled when the sign comes down and will want to read all the books in the box.

Stackable Portfolios
Ask a local pizzeria to donate a large unused pizza box for each child in your class. Have students write their names along the sides of the boxes and decorate them as desired. Stack the boxes against a wall. The boxes can easily accommodate artwork and large projects that do not fit in regular folders.

Honorable Letterhead
Make honor roll students feel special with their own letterhead. Write or type the student's name across a blank label. Under it write "Honor Roll Student" and your school name. Attach the label to the top of a sheet of plain paper and photocopy several sheets for the student. Keep the original to make additional copies when needed.

Homework Calendar
Eliminate the "I didn't know about the homework" excuse with this calendar. Divide a large piece of white poster board into five rows and seven columns and laminate. Add month and day labels and fill in the dates. Each day, write the homework assignments in the correct block on the calendar. Display the poster board until the month is filled in so students know what assignments are due.

Bag It!
Make the distribution of textbooks a breeze by grouping book sets in paper or plastic grocery bags. Write a single number on the bag and make a master list of the book numbers in each bag. Then, each year record which bag each child is assigned. Last year's students can also leave messages, treats, etc., in their bags for next year's students.

Take a Number!
Help students in an orderly fashion. Number index cards from one to the number of students in the classroom, and place upright in a box on your desk. Have students take numbers from the front of the box and place them on their desks so you can see who is next in line for help. After answering a student's question, return his card to the back of the box.

May

Day-by-Day Calendar

1 **Mother Goose Day** Have students skip rope while chanting Mother Goose rhymes.

2 **National Pet Week** is the first full week in May. Invite students to bring in photos or drawings of their pets.

3 **National Hamburger Month** Go on a field trip to a local fast food restaurant for a tour and hamburgers!

4 **National Teacher Day** is the Tuesday of the first full week in May. Let students make cards thanking teachers for their hard work.

5 **Leo Lionni's Birthday** The children's author was born today in 1910. Share one of his books, such as *Alexander and the Wind-Up Mouse* or *Swimmy*.

6 The **world's first postage stamp** was **issued** in England today in 1840. Have students design their own stamps in honor of the occasion. Designs for postage stamps can be much larger than the final product. Hold a class-wide competition for the best design.

7 **Cartoon Art Appreciation Week** is May 1-7. Have a cartoon *Show and Tell* with the class. Have students bring in items that depict their favorite cartoon characters, such as stuffed animals, comic books, lunch boxes, etc.

8 **No Socks Day** Invite students to take off their socks in honor of this day.

9 **Jean de Brunhoff's Birthday** The creator of Babar was born on this day in 1899. Have students pick an animal and write a short adventure story about it.

10 **National Etiquette Week** begins on Monday in the second week of May. Make a *We Have Good Manners!* bulletin board. Have students draw pictures depicting good manners.

11 **Irving Berlin's Birthday** The song writer was born in 1888. Sing or play one of his songs, such as *God Bless America* or *White Christmas*.

12 **Limerick Day** Share limericks with the class. Have older students try their hands at writing poems in this style.

13 **Electrical Safety Month** Brainstorm safety rules to use when dealing with electricity such as, *Never use an electrical appliance around water*. Post the rules in the classroom.

14 **National Salad Month** Have a salad taste test. Bring in different varieties of salad, such as fruit, Caesar, chicken, etc. Record which salad most students liked best.

15 **Physical Fitness/Sports Month** Have students do several minutes of physical exercise each day this month such as jogging, jumping jacks, etc.

4

16 *National New Friends, Old Friends Week* is May 16–22. Divide students into small groups. Have each member of each group tell an anecdote about something they experienced with a friend.

17 *National Sight-Saving Month* Invite an ophthalmologist or optometrist to talk with students about ways to take care of their eyes.

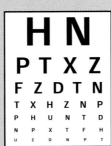

18 *International Museum Day* If it is not possible to visit a museum, bring in photographs of works of art (paintings, sculptures, etc.) to share with the class.

19 *May Ray Day* Celebrate the warm days of May by taking students outside and letting them sit on blankets for a read-aloud story.

20 *Amelia Earhart began flying across the Atlantic* today in 1932. Teach the class some facts about this amazing pilot, such as she was born on July 24, 1897 and she earned her pilot's license in 1932.

21 *International Pickle Week* is May 21–31. Bring in sweet, sour, hot, fruit, and vegetable versions of pickles and have a pickle party.

22 *National Salsa Month* Make salsa with the class to enjoy with tortilla chips as an afternoon snack.

23 *Older Americans Month* Have students make cards to deliver to a rest home in your area.

24 *National Backyard Games Week* ends on Memorial Day. Play softball, volleyball, etc., in honor of this week.

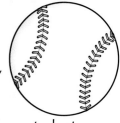

25 *Breathe Easy Month* Have students research ways to keep their lungs healthy.

26 *National Egg Month* Make a list of ways that eggs can be prepared as well as foods that contain eggs. Then, take a class survey of favorites and graph the results.

27  *The Golden Gate Bridge opened* today in 1937. Teach the class facts about the Golden Gate Bridge. If possible, bring in photos to share.

28 *The Sierra Club* was *founded* today in 1892. Explain that the Sierra Club is an environmental organization dedicated to protecting the Earth. Brainstorm ways to help this cause.

29 *International Jazz Day* is the Saturday of Memorial Day weekend. Bring in jazz music to share with the class.

30 *Better Sleep Month* Brainstorm a list of benefits from getting a good night's sleep. Have students draw pictures to pair with the statements. Bind the pictures in a class book and let each student take it home to enjoy as a bedtime story.

31 *National Barbecue Month* Have students plan menus for the ideal barbecue—then write and decorate their menus on construction paper.

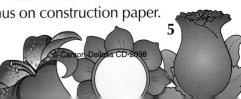

	Sunday	Monday	Tuesday	Wednesday	Thursday	Friday	Saturday
May							

May Gazette

Teacher _____ Date _____

IN THE NEWS

TAKE NOTE

WHAT'S COMING UP

KID'S CORNER   Connect the dots.

Celebrate May!

Dear Family Members,
Here are a few quick-and-easy activities to help you and your child celebrate special days throughout the month of May.

May 1 is *Mother Goose Day*
- See how many Mother Goose rhymes you and your child can name. Recite several of your favorites together.

May is *National Strawberry Month*
- Honor this occasion by making delicious chocolate-covered strawberries. Melt a package of chocolate chips according to package directions. Place a strawberry on the end of a fork and carefully dip it halfway into the melted chocolate. Place the strawberries on waxed paper until the chocolate sets.

May is *Electrical Safety Month*
- Remind children how to be safe around electrical outlets and appliances. Review the following rules:
  - Never put fingers or other objects into electrical sockets.
  - Never touch outside power lines, especially if they are on the ground.
  - Do not overload electrical sockets.
  - Do not use appliances that have frayed cords.
  - Never use electrical appliances near water.

May 18 is *International Museum Day*
- Visit a local museum with your child. After the trip, have your child draw a picture of a favorite thing he or she saw.

May is *National Salsa Month*
- Enjoy salsa with chips as a special snack.
  - 4 cans of whole tomatoes, drained and chopped
  - 1 large onion, chopped
  - 1 small can jalapeños, drained
  - 1 large can green chiles, drained
  - 1 tsp. garlic
  - 1/2 tsp. salt
  - 1/2 tsp. pepper
  - Juice from 4 limes
  - 1 1/2 tsp. cilantro
  - 1 tsp. chili powder

Place all ingredients in a bowl and stir until well blended.
Serve with chips. Makes about 8 cups.

National Backyard Games Week ends on Memorial Day
- Play a backyard game such as horseshoes, croquet, or badminton with your family.

Read In May!

Dear Family Members,
Here are some books to share with your child to enhance the enjoyment of reading in May.

 The Summer My Father Was Ten by Pat Brisson
- *A girl's father tells her about a time he carelessly ruined a neighbor's garden. He eventually apologized and helped the neighbor grow a new garden the next year.*
- After reading the story, discuss the importance of respecting others' property, apologizing, and making amends.

 Fireflies for Nathan by Shulamith Levey Oppenheim
- *When Nathan visits his grandparents, they help him catch fireflies like they did with his father when he was young.*
- Read the story, then go outside at twilight and try to catch fireflies. Catch them in your hands and let them go, or put them in a jar with holes punched in the lid and observe them. Remember to set the fireflies free.

 Around the Pond: Who's Been Here? by Lindsay Barrett George
- *A brother and sister walk around a pond and discover clues to the many animals that have been there.*
- After reading the story, take a nature walk around your house or in a park. Look for clues left behind by animals. Speculate with your child about who has been there.

 The Butterfly House by Eve Bunting
- *A girl's grandfather helps her make a home for a caterpillar. When the caterpillar becomes a butterfly, they release it.*
- Help your child decorate a shoe box as a butterfly house. Then, look in a field guide and draw pictures of several butterflies that could be found in your area of the country. Cut out the butterflies and tape a length of thread to each butterfly. Tape the threads to the top of the box so the butterflies appear to be flying in the box.

 Allison's Zinnias by Anita Lobel
- *Beautiful paintings introduce readers to a variety of flowers in an alphabet book format.*
- Read the book, then go outside. For each letter of the alphabet, challenge your child to name something he or she sees in nature.

Flower Garden by Eve Bunting
- *A little girl and her father buy flowering plants and create a window box garden.*
- Plan to visit a garden shop or the garden section of a large store with your child. Locate the things you would need to buy to make a window box. If possible, buy the items and plant a window box to display at your child's bedroom window or another window in your home.

THREE CHEERS FOR YOU!

Name _____

Signed _____

Date _____

© Carson-Dellosa CD-2098

_____ can

"Bee" Proud!

"Bee" cause _____

_____

Signed _____

Date _____

© Carson-Dellosa CD-2098

10

_____ shows

Tremendous Teamwork!

Signed _____ **Date** _____

_____ does

Blooming Good Work!

Signed _____

Date _____

MAY
Writing Activities

Springtime is the best time for writing! Spruce up your writing exercises with these fresh ideas for classroom writing!

Lights, camera, action! Have students reflect on the past school year and make video journals to share with their parents and upcoming classes. Let each student write a journal entry about events, activities, or friends made during the year. Videotape each student as he reads his journal entry aloud.

Word Bank Words

grasshopper	pond	flower
roots	grow	garden
sprouts	soil	frog
tadpole	dragonfly	ladybug
seeds	lily pad	firefly

Line Editing Made Easy

Provide green- and white-lined computer

paper for students to use for early writing

Good Idea!

drafts. Instruct students to write on the white

lines. When the drafts are passed to classmates

for editing, have the editors write their

Use a red pen.

comments in the green spaces of each line.

Interview with a Classmate

Teach students to learn by asking! Pair students and have one act as an interviewer and the other as the interviewee. Have students write questions covering topics such as favorite activities, family members, etc. Instruct students to write down the answers as they receive them. After the interview, have students switch places. Let each interviewer present his profile to the class.

Guess Which One

Practice descriptive writing with May flowers and vegetables! Have each student choose a flower or vegetable and write a description of its color, shape, texture, and size. Let each student read his description to the class and then have the class try to guess the flower or vegetable being described.

Never the Same Way Twice

Practice inventive spelling! When writing spelling words for practice, provide materials and suggestions for students to use so they are never writing spelling words the same way twice. Students can write words in pencil, pen, crayon, or markers. They can use all capital letters, cursive, print, bubble letters, or type the words on a computer. Challenge students to use a different method each time!

cool COOL **cool**

LITTLE *little* little

bright BRIGHT bright

tree TREE *tree*

We Want to Learn

Letter writing leads to learning! Before a field trip, encourage students to write letters to the destination (zoo, fire station, etc.). Instruct students to describe what they know about the place and what they want to learn. Send the letters, but keep copies for the students to view after the trip to see what they have learned.

Jane Miller
56 Park Lane
Smithfield, NY 10002

Main Street Fire Department
72 Main Street
Smithfield, NY 10002

What's Behind the Door?

Knock-knock! Find out who's there by having students decorate a piece of paper to resemble a door. Staple this page over a sheet of writing paper. Have students write about who is behind the door.

Every living thing likes to sing in spring!

The flowers seem to say "Come out, it's time to play!"

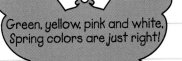

Green, yellow, pink and white, Spring colors are just right!

May Couplet Mobiles

Let budding poets create spring rhymes. Have students choose a springtime topic and write two-line couplets about the chosen theme. Explain that a couplet is two lines whose ending words rhyme. Let students draw, cut out, and decorate springtime shapes and then write poems on them. Punch a hole in the top of each shape and use yarn to connect the poems in groups of three. Hang from the ceiling or on a spring bulletin board.

Bulletin Board Ideas

Keep everyone informed of class activities with this display! Draw a large beehive shape, cut it out, and attach it to the board over green paper cut to resemble grass. Give each student a copy of the honeybee pattern (page 32) to color and cut out. Label the bees with student names. Write upcoming class events and activities on enlarged flower patterns (page 44). Provide a hexagon template with 2" sides and let students trace and cut the six-sided shapes from yellow paper. Let students connect the shapes to make a honeycomb border. Title the bulletin board *We Are Busy Bees!* and display during your study of *Bugs, Bees, and Butterflies* (pages 20-34).

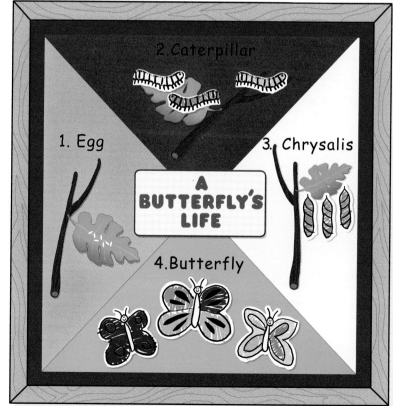

Use this larger than life display to help students learn the life cycle of a butterfly. Cover the board with colorful paper and divide into four sections. Number and label the sections *Egg, Caterpillar, Chrysalis,* and *Butterfly*. Glue sticks and real leaves in the first three sections. Glue grains of rice to the leaf in the first section to represent eggs. Have students draw and cut out caterpillars, chrysalises, and butterflies to display in the other sections. Suspend the butterflies with nylon string if desired. This bulletin board complements the *Bugs, Bees, and Butterflies* chapter (page 20-34).

Insects have three body parts: head, thorax, and abdomen.

Insects have six legs.

Insects have two wings.

Most insects have two wings.

Some insects have four wings.

Insects have two antennae.

Some insects have stingers.   Most insects have two large eyes.

BUGS, BUGS, BUGS!

Create a creepy, crawly display to teach students about insects. Begin by writing facts about insects on 3"-wide strips of poster board. Border the display with these strips. Have students use this information to draw, color, and cut out their own insects to display on the board. Add other crafts made during your study of the *Bugs, Bees, and Butterflies* chapter (pages 20-34).

WHAT'S IN THE GARDEN?

Plant a bulletin board flower garden complete with visitors. Cover the bottom of the board with brown paper, the top with blue paper, and accent with white "clouds." Give students enlarged copies of the flower patterns (page 44) to color and cut out. Use green paper to cut stems, leaves, and vines to attach to the patterns so they resemble a growing garden. Cut flaps in the patterns and have students draw garden creatures hiding among the plants. Close the flaps and let students guess what is in the garden! Display this bulletin board during your study of the *What's in the Garden?* chapter (pages 35-45).

15

Create a garden of smiles with this display. Cover the board with sky-blue paper and shades of green paper cut to resemble grass. Give each student a copy of the sunflower pattern (page 44) on which to draw a self-portrait. Glue real sunflower seeds around the portraits. Post the flowers on the bulletin board for a bright and sunny display during your study of the *What's in the Garden?* chapter (pages 35-45).

Students will reel in facts about pond life with this display. Cover the board with blue paper. Cover the bottom 2/3 with blue plastic wrap for a watery look. Draw and cut out several fish, writing a pond life fact on each one. Attach one end of a piece of yarn to each fish and the other end to fishing poles cut from paper. Enhance the display with cattails, lily pads, and dragonflies made in the *Exploring Pond Life* chapter (pages 62-75).

Keep your class hopping with this incentive idea. Cut out several lily pad shapes from green paper and post them on the board. Write a class goal on each lily pad. Give each student a frog pattern (page 73) to color, cut out, and personalize. When daily goals are met, use push pins to move the frogs to the appropriate lily pads. Accent the display with the *Lovely Lillies* from the *Exploring Pond Life* chapter (pages 62-75).

Use this crafty display to help children learn where different pond animals and plants live and grow. Cut a large pond shape from shades of blue paper and post it on one side of the board. Cover the remaining board with green paper cut to resemble grass and sky-blue paper with white "clouds." Have students draw appropriate animals and plants on, in, and around the pond. This display complements the *Exploring Pond Life* chapter (pages 62-75).

Let students introduce their families and interests to the class with this bulletin board display. Give each child a piece of white paper on which to draw a family portrait. Provide colorful paper for the frame. Have students cut and decorate the frames to represent a family interest such as tennis, camping, etc. Cut the portrait to fit and attach to the center of the "frame." If desired, post the family portraits on a board framed with a wood grain border. Use this display during *Celebrate the Family* (pages 88-92).

OUR FAMILIES

- Alan's Family
- Jasmine's Family
- Michael's Family
- Eric's Family
- Shandra's Family
- Becky's Family
- Justin's Family
- Juanita's Family

PICK OF THE PATCH

Highlight sweet student work with this display idea. Give each student a copy of the strawberry pattern (page 49) to color and cut out. Post the strawberries on the board to accent student work. Cut leaves from green paper and use twisted green paper to border the bulletin board and connect the strawberries. This strawberry patch display complements the *Delightful, Delicious Berries* chapter (pages 46-49).

STARRY NIGHT

Can you name these constellations?

Encourage students to search the night sky for constellations. Cover the board with black paper. Draw constellations on the paper using glow-in-the-dark chalk or paint. Turn off the lights and let children try to identify them. After a few days, label the constellations and post new ones for the class to identify. This bulletin board complements the *Star Gazing* chapter (pages 82-87).

BRIGHT AND SHINING WORK

Make your students feel like All-Stars with this display. Let students trace and cut out large star shapes. Have them paint the stars with a thin layer of glue, then sprinkle with gold glitter. Use the shining stars to highlight student work. Give groups of students 2' x 3" strips of poster board to create a border. Have students decorate the strips with stars, moons, "shooting stars," comets, etc. This display works well during your study of *Star Gazing* (pages 82-87).

BUGS, BEES, AND BUTTERFLIES

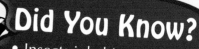

Turn your students into insect experts with these creepy, crawly bug activities.

Literature Selections

Bugs by Nancy Winslow Parker: William Morrow & Company, 1987. (Picture book, 40 pg.) Delightful couplets are used to describe sixteen insects.

Fireflies for Nathan by Shulamith Levey Oppenheim: Tambourine, 1994. (Picture book, 32 pg.) A boy's grandparents help him catch fireflies like they did with his father when he was young.

Insects Are My Life by Megan McDonald: Orchard Books, 1995. (Picture book, 32 pg.) Amanda loves collecting and studying insects.

The 512 Ants on Sullivan Street by Carol A. Losi: Scholastic, 1997. (Picture book, 48 pg.) The number of ants multiplies as they take treats from a picnic lunch.

The Little Red Ant and the Great Big Crumb by Shirley Climo: Clarion Books, 1999. (Picture book, 40 pg.) An ant searches for someone to help him carry a large crumb.

What Makes a Bug a Bug?

These creepy creations will teach students the adaptations of insects. On sentence strips, write sentences describing insect features with the heading *Insects*. On another set of sentence strips, list special adaptations that only some insects have, such as four wings. Post these with the heading *Special Features*. Then, give each child modeling clay, a pipe cleaner, two round-end toothpicks, and a small piece of paper. Have students create insects that have all the features listed under the *Insects* heading. Children can customize their creations by adding features listed under the *Special Features* heading. Have students name the parts of an insect on a model.

Insects
Insects have three body parts:
    the head, the thorax, and the abdomen.
Insects have six legs.
Most insects have two wings.
Insects have two antennae.
Most insects have two large eyes.

Special Features
Some insects have four wings.
Some insects have stingers.
Some insects have brightly-colored wings.
Some insects have several smaller eyes.

Through the Eyes of an Insect

Explore an insect's compound eye with puzzle pieces. Most insects have two large, compound eyes and several smaller simple eyes. The simple eyes differentiate between light and dark and the compound eyes focus on objects. Because an insect is unable to move its eyes, its compound eye contains many *ommatidia* (ah•muh•TI•dee•uh) or lenses, that each focus on part of an object. Help students understand this by cutting a large poster or magazine picture into several pieces. Give each child a piece of the picture and then have students work together to assemble the pieces. Explain that each piece of the puzzle represents what each lens sees.

Walk Like an Insect

Students will enjoy "walking the walk" of an insect! Insects balance on three legs at a time by placing the front and hind legs of one side and the middle leg of the opposite side on the ground. Divide the class into groups of three. Have students stand in a line with their hands on the shoulders of the person in front of them. Place a yellow dot on the left shoe of the first and last person in line. Put a yellow dot on the right shoe of the middle person. Place red dots on the other three shoes. Call out a color and have children take a step forward using the correct foot. Then, call out the other color and have students step forward with the other foot. Alternately call out colors until students are walking like six-legged insects.

A Home Fit for an Ant

Who would guess that beneath a tiny ant hill lies an entire ant city! Have children design ant nests on file folders by drawing an ant hill shape at the top of the folder. Color the ant hill brown and draw grass, flowers, etc. On the inside, draw and label different parts of a nest, connecting them with tunnels. Finally, draw busy ants at work. On the bottom half of the folder, have students write about how ants build their nests and live and work inside them. Explain that the ant hill above the ground is made of the grains of earth the ants carry up from below when building their nests. The bigger an ant hill is, the larger the ant nest below. An ant nest has many chambers which each serve a specific purpose. One chamber is for the queen and her eggs. Other chambers are nurseries, where workers care for young ants. Seeds are stored in a special food chamber deep in the ground to protect them from other insects and animals. Ants winter in the deepest (and warmest) chambers of the nest. If possible, purchase a self-contained ant farm for students to view.

Nurseries

Workers' resting rooms

The Queen's room

Seed storage rooms

Winter rooms

Ant hills are made when ants pile up dirt they dig out of the ground when making tunnels and rooms. The Queen sits in her room laying eggs all day. Worker ants gather and store food, look after baby ants in the nurseries, and help the Queen. Sometimes the worker ants need to take a break, so there are resting rooms for them. Ants sleep in rooms at the bottom of the nest during the winter. Worker ants are always building, digging, and repairing rooms and tunnels in the nest as the colony gets bigger and bigger.

BUTTERFLIES

Nothing brightens up the springtime sky quite like a butterfly. Introduce students to these amazing, delicate creatures.

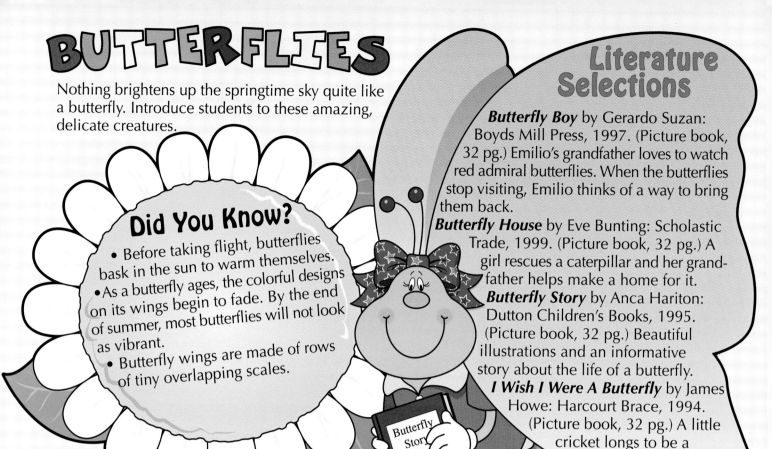

Did You Know?

• Before taking flight, butterflies bask in the sun to warm themselves.
• As a butterfly ages, the colorful designs on its wings begin to fade. By the end of summer, most butterflies will not look as vibrant.
• Butterfly wings are made of rows of tiny overlapping scales.

Literature Selections

Butterfly Boy by Gerardo Suzan: Boyds Mill Press, 1997. (Picture book, 32 pg.) Emilio's grandfather loves to watch red admiral butterflies. When the butterflies stop visiting, Emilio thinks of a way to bring them back.
Butterfly House by Eve Bunting: Scholastic Trade, 1999. (Picture book, 32 pg.) A girl rescues a caterpillar and her grandfather helps make a home for it.
Butterfly Story by Anca Hariton: Dutton Children's Books, 1995. (Picture book, 32 pg.) Beautiful illustrations and an informative story about the life of a butterfly.
I Wish I Were A Butterfly by James Howe: Harcourt Brace, 1994. (Picture book, 32 pg.) A little cricket longs to be a beautiful butterfly.

Butterfly or Moth?

Display the differences between butterflies and moths on mobiles! Pair students and provide reference materials about butterflies and moths. Assign one child to research four facts about butterflies and another to research four facts about moths. Give each student four copies of the butterfly or moth pattern (page 33) to color and cut out. Instruct students to write one fact about their assigned insect on each of the patterns. Students can make mobiles using the patterns, various lengths of yarn, and pipe cleaners. Give each student two pipe cleaners to twist together in an "X" shape. Create a hanger with a loop of yarn.

Butterflies

• Are active mostly during the day
• Usually have brightly colored wings
• Fold wings up over their backs when resting
• Have long and thin antennae with club shapes on the ends
• Create a pupa without silk that is called a chrysalis
• Have little hair on their bodies and antennae

Moths

• Are active mostly at dusk or at night
• Usually have dull colored wings
• Hold wings outward and flat when resting
• Have feathery or plain antennae
• Create a pupa with silk called a cocoon
• Have lots of hair on their bodies and antennae

Sip Like a Butterfly

Take a sip like a butterfly with this fun and easy craft! A butterfly has a long feeding tube (proboscis) that it uncoils when it sips nectar. Give each child a small paper or plastic cup. Place the cup upside down on paper and trace around the top. Instruct each student to draw a flower shape around the circle, color it, and cut it out. Cut an "X" in the center of the circle and push the pattern up from the bottom of the cup. Tape the flaps to the cup below the flower. Fill each cup halfway with juice. Give each child two or three flexible drinking straws and instruct them to tuck the end of one straw into the end of another to make one long straw. Have each student use his straw to drink the juice just like a butterfly uses its proboscis to sip nectar.

Butterfly Life Cycle

Make a butterfly's life cycle "crystal" clear with this activity. A butterfly begins life as a tiny egg from which a caterpillar hatches. The caterpillar feeds on plants and grows very quickly before shedding its skin, or molting, to allow room for growth. Young caterpillars are usually green but turn brown closer to the pupa stage. In the pupa stage, the caterpillar attaches itself to a plant and covers itself with a chrysalis. (Moth caterpillars form cocoons.) A butterfly emerges from the chrysalis. Copy the Butterfly Life Cycle pattern (page 34) and have children illustrate each stage by coloring the patterns and adding the details noted in the diagram at right.

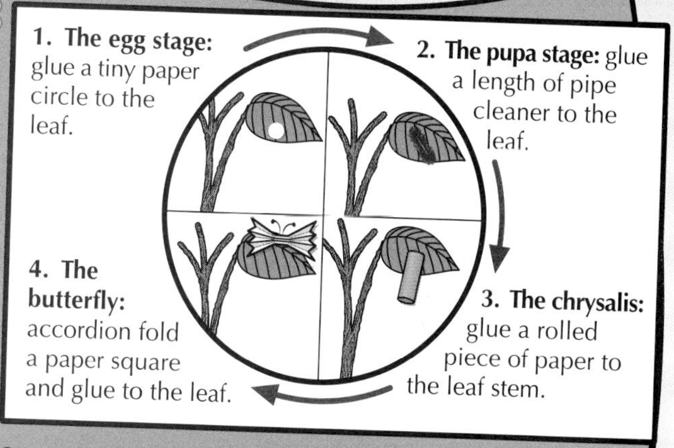

1. **The egg stage:** glue a tiny paper circle to the leaf.

2. **The pupa stage:** glue a length of pipe cleaner to the leaf.

3. **The chrysalis:** glue a rolled piece of paper to the leaf stem.

4. **The butterfly:** accordion fold a paper square and glue to the leaf.

From Caterpillar to Butterfly

Students can make caterpillars which, with a little help, will be transformed into beautiful butterflies! Give each child a small cardboard tube and have him decorate it to resemble a caterpillar. Make a chrysalis for the caterpillar by gluing the tube in the middle of a piece of paper. Instruct the children to wrap and tape the paper around the caterpillar. Have students leave their projects in the classroom overnight. When students have gone, open each chrysalis and draw butterfly wings on the paper around the caterpillar, then tape it closed again. The next day, when each student opens his chrysalis he will be surprised to see that the caterpillar has changed into a beautiful butterfly! Let students color their butterfly's wings, cut them out, and display them around the room.

23

Where's the Butterfly?

Students will understand camouflage when they don't see it with their own eyes! The top of a butterfly's wings is usually brightly-colored, while the underside is dull. Demonstrate camouflage by having students fold a paper in half and draw a wing shape along the fold. Cut through both papers without cutting on the fold. Open the wings and make colorful designs on the top of the pattern and color the underside a muted color such as green or brown. Give each child a wooden clothespin (the spindle type) and have her color it black. Slide the wings on the clothespin and glue in place. Have each student cut a leaf shape from green paper. Demonstrate protective coloring by placing the butterfly on the leaf with its wings open and note how easy it is to see. Then, pinch the tops of the wings together to see how the dull color makes the butterfly more difficult to see.

Butterfly Treats

These treats are sure to cause a flutter of excitement. On a paper plate, give each child two pretzel twists, a spoonful of prepared cake icing, and a small piece of licorice. Attach the bottoms of the pretzels together with icing to create butterfly wings. To make the antennae, place two small licorice pieces at the top of the butterfly.

A Butterfly Guide

Butterflies add a touch of beauty to the summer sky. With a class field guide, students can learn to recognize different butterflies. Explain that butterfly watchers use pictures to identify butterflies. Let each child draw a butterfly of his choice on white paper. Students can tear or cut small pieces of colored construction or tissue paper to glue to the butterfly for a mosaic effect. Under the illustration, have him write the name of the butterfly and where it can be found. Combine all the pages to create a class field guide.

Orange Sulphur (Colia eurytheme) Southern Canada to Mexico and most of the United States

Butterfly Finger Puppets

Create a room full of fluttering butterflies! Using the butterfly pattern (page 33), have students make fluttering butterflies. Let each student color and cut out the pattern. Give each student a strip of construction paper approximately 3" long and 1" wide. Have her wrap the strip around her index finger and tape it closed. Then, attach the paper strip to the pattern. Have each child put the rolled paper on her finger and gently move her arm up and down. Explain that butterfly wings look delicate, but are actually quite strong. They contain a framework of veins that supports the wings just as rods support a kite.

GRASSHOPPERS & CRICKETS

Cricket and Grasshopper Songs

Crickets and grasshoppers have a special ability most other insects do not have—they can sing! Grasshoppers make buzzing sounds by rubbing one hind leg against a wing or by rubbing their wings together. Crickets make chirping sounds by rubbing their wings together. Each species of cricket has its own song, so crickets from different groups can easily find each other. Have children pretend to be grasshoppers and crickets and use their hands (wings) to make distinct sounds. Students can clap, snap fingers, rub hands together, etc. Let children share their insect songs with the class.

Hungry Grasshoppers and Crickets

Snack time is the right time to discover how insects eat! Insects do not have teeth, but grasshoppers and crickets do have special mouth parts to chew foods like leaves, grass, and seeds. Rough ridges on their powerful jaws enable these insects to chew their food. Use this demonstration to illustrate how these adaptations work. Show students a pair of pliers. Open the pliers and let students feel the rough ridges on the inside. Explain that the pliers open and close in a side-to-side motion like the mouth parts of grasshoppers and crickets. Give each student a carrot or celery stick to chew. Have each child put his hand under his jaw and feel the up-and-down motion of his mouth as he chews. Compare how a person chews food differently than an insect.

Cricket Thermometers

Teach students to count cricket chirps to determine the temperature of a spring evening! Crickets and grasshoppers are more active and vocal in warm weather. When the evening temperature is below 55° F, crickets are silent. Ask students to do a little "field" work for homework. To find the temperature in Fahrenheit, have students count the number of cricket chirps they hear in 15 seconds. Write down the number of chirps, then add 40 to the number. This number is the temperature in Fahrenheit. For example, if your hear 33 chirps in 15 seconds, you would add 40 to 33 to get 73° F. Have students use an outdoor thermometer to test the accuracy of their results. Let students share their findings with the class the following day. To complete this activity in school, tape record the sound of crickets and let students determine what the temperature was that evening. If a tape recording is not possible, use a whistle or object that makes a clicking noise.

LADYBUGS

There's a Ladybug on the Ceiling!

How can insects walk on walls and ceilings? Let students discover the secret using the following activity. Explain that flies have moisture on their feet and ladybugs have special sticky pads on their feet that enable them to stick to walls and ceilings. Let students make upside-down ladybugs using copies of the ladybug pattern (page 32). Have each student cut out the pattern and fold where indicated. Use a paintbrush to apply a small amount of water to the ladybug's feet. Place the ladybug on the bottom of a glass mug, a plastic container lid, or a paper plate. Turn the object upside-down to see how the ladybug sticks to the surface. Explain that moisture from the water on the ladybug's feet helped it stick to the surface just like the sticky pads on an actual ladybug's feet.

Dear Ladybug,
    Thank you for keeping aphids away from the flowers in my garden. You are my favorite bug!
    Your friend,
    Lucy

Thank You, Ladybug

Let students write thank-you notes to our beneficial friend—the ladybug! Ladybugs are among the group of insects called "beneficials" by farmers and gardeners because they eat harmful insects that would otherwise damage crops. In the 1800s, an insect pest began attacking orange trees in California. Five hundred ladybugs were sent to California to feed on these insects which saved the orange trees from being destroyed. Have children write and illustrate thank-you letters to the ladybug for helping protect crops and gardens. Provide red cinnamon candies for students to glue in their garden scenes and decorate them as hard-working ladybugs.

Fly Ladybug, Fly!

Students will discover how a ladybug protects its delicate wings when they make these crafts. Ladybugs are known for their brightly-colored spotted "wings." But these reddish-orange parts are actually wing covers that protect the wings. The wing covers open, but do not move, during flight. When a ladybug lands, it carefully tucks its wings under the covers. Instruct students to cut one red circle and one black circle from paper to represent the wing covers and body. Cut another circle from white tissue paper. Cut this and the red circle in half. Cut a smaller circle from black paper to represent the ladybug's head. Let students decorate the red wing covers with black dots. Use two paper fasteners to attach the three layers. Have each student glue the smaller circle to the top of the ladybug and decorate it. Students can open the ladybug wings and wing covers and write facts about ladybugs inside with white colored pencils or crayons.

* Ladybugs eat aphids.
* Ladybugs have sticky feet that let them walk on the ceiling!
* Not all ladybugs are red.
* Ladybugs' wings tuck under their red wing covers when not in use.

FIREFLIES

Flashing Fireflies

Create a room full of twinkling fireflies! **1.** Have each student color and cut out the firefly pattern (page 32). Cut out the inside of the firefly pattern where indicated. Instruct students to trace and cut out the firefly pattern from black construction paper. Give each child a copy of the firefly light pattern (page 32) to color yellow and cut out (use glow in the dark paint, if possible). **2.** On the back of the black paper firefly, an adult can use a craft knife to cut a horizontal slit as wide as the widest point on the firefly light pattern. Apply glue around the edges of the colored firefly and glue it to the black paper firefly. **3.** Slide the firefly light pattern into the slit. To make the fireflies twinkle, have students pull the tabs on the back of fireflies up and down. To enhance this activity, read Eric Carle's (battery operated) book, *The Very Lonely Firefly*, and enjoy the surprise twinkles on the last page.

Collecting Jars

Get a close-up view of your object of study when students make and use collecting jars. Have parents send in empty, clean plastic jars with lids. Students can make labels to glue to the fronts and then copy the *Tips for Bug Collecting* (below) to place in their jars. Let students take the jars home for "bugwork." Students can bring a firefly or other insect to school for a day and then take it home to release it.

Tips for Bug Collecting

- Punch air holes in a jar lid. Gently hold the jar over the bug and slide the lid underneath it. Place the lid on jar.
- Do not touch the bug.
- Add twigs, leaves, and moist grass to the jar to make it more inviting for the bug.
- Look at bugs with a magnifying glass. Try to identify the bug using a field guide.
- Don't touch bees, centipedes, spiders, or other bugs that can bite or sting.
- Keep the bug for a day or two, then let it go in the spot where you found it.

Secret Firefly Messages

Twinkling fireflies are communicating when they light up the summer sky. Each species has its own flashing signal, which it uses to attract other fireflies. Have students create firefly messages using flashlights. Provide two flashlights. Let one student turn a flashlight on and off to create a code. Then, have another student use his flashlight to repeat the message back. Allow students to take turns sending and repeating messages to each other with the flashlights.

HONEYBEES

Few insects work as hard as the honeybee. From gathering pollen and nectar to building intricate hives, the honeybee is always busy. Give students a glimpse into the life of these amazing insects.

Did You Know?

- A colony of honeybees gathers nectar from approximately one million flowers to make one pound of honey.
- The first honeybees were brought to America by Pilgrims in 1638.
- Honeybees see ultraviolet light, which humans cannot. This ultraviolet vision enables honeybees to see dark shapes on flower petals, indicating nectar inside.

Literature Selections

Beekeepers by Linda Oatman High: Boyds Mills Press, 1998. (Picture book, 32 pg.) A girl helps her grandfather tend his bees.

Gran's Bees by Mary Thompson: Millbrook Press, 1996. (Picture book, 32 pg.) Jessie and her dad help her grandmother harvest honey. Includes factual information about bees and beekeeping.

Mr. Bumble by Kim Kennedy: Disney Press, 1997. (Picture book, 32 pg.) Clumsy Mr. Bumble learns how to gracefully gather honey.

The Bee Tree by Patricia Polacco: Philomel Books, 1993. (Picture book, 32 pg.) Mary Ellen and her grandfather lead the townspeople on a honeybee chase, ending with the characters gathering honey from the hive.

The Honey Makers by Gail Gibbons: Morrow Junior Books, 1997. (Picture book, 32 pg.) Describes in detailed text and illustrations how honeybees live, build hives, and produce honey.

Honeycomb Hives

Get students busy gathering honeybee facts for this honeycomb activity. Explain that the inside of a honeybee hive is made up of thousands of six-sided sections. These sections, or cells, are made from beeswax, a substance which bees make inside their bodies. Bring in beeswax candles and chunk honey (honey with a piece of comb in it) so students can see these objects firsthand. The honeycomb cells are used to store honey and pollen—food for the honeybees. Bee larvae (baby honeybees) are also stored in some cells of the honeycomb. Create a class honeycomb by having students use rulers to measure 4½" lines and draw hexagon shapes on yellow paper. Give each child six craft sticks and let him use a marker to color the sticks yellow. Students can cut out the shapes, and then stand the craft sticks up to glue the edges to the hexagons to create a honeycomb section. When dry, provide reference and have students write facts about honeybees on the sections. Staple the sections to a bulletin board to form a large honeycomb.

Honeybees eat honey for energy.

Honeybees build comb from wax that comes from their bodies.

Honeybees dance to tell other bees where to find flowers.

Chores for Honeybees

Honeybees wrote the book on job assignments—let students illustrate it! Explain that house bees remain inside the hive. They clean the hive, build the comb, store the food, and protect the hive from enemies. Field bees gather nectar and pollen and collect water from puddles to thin the honey and to cool the hive in summer. Sap from plants is collected by field bees and is used to seal and protect the walls of the hive. Draw and cut out a large hive shape from butcher paper. Post the hive on a classroom wall or bulletin board. Have students draw a field of flowers outside the hive. Label the hive *House Bees* and the field of flowers *Field Bees*. Let students draw and cut out honeybees and write facts about each bee and its duties. Put the house bees inside the hive and the field bees in the field of flowers. Refer to *A Home Fit for an Ant* (page 21) to compare and contrast the job assignments in bee hives and ant colonies.

Do a Little Dance

Students can learn interpretive dance from the honeybee! Field bees work from sunrise until sunset gathering nectar and pollen from about 10,000 flowers a day. When a honeybee finds a supply of nectar, it uses special dances to tell the other honeybees where to find the nectar. These dances show the direction and distance of the flowers from the hive. Let students imitate two bee dances. Using the diagram below, place masking tape on the floor and draw arrows indicating how students should move to do a bee dance. As the class does each bee dance, have them interpret what it means in honeybee language!

Round Dance

This dance tells the other bees that flowers are within 100 yards of the hive. The bee makes a circle in one direction, then turns around and circles back in the opposite direction. The other bees fly in a circular motion around the hive until they find the flowers.

Tail-Wagging Dance

This dance tells that the flowers are far away and in which direction to fly. The bee moves in a half-circle in one direction, then runs straight ahead while wagging its body. The faster the bee wags its body, the farther away the food is. Then the bee moves in a half-circle in the opposite direction. The bee wags either to the left or right to indicate where the flowers are in relation to the sun. If the bee holds her back end straight up, the flowers are toward the sun.

29

Be a Beekeeper

Students can use copies of the *Be a Beekeeper* worksheet (page 31) to display their knowledge of apiculture—beekeeping! Beekeepers help honeybees survive cold winters, blazing summer temperatures, and honey thieves like bears and skunks. Honeybees are kept in box-shaped hives (an apiary) that are made of stackable sections. The sections contain wooden frames where the honeycomb is built. For protection from stings, beekeepers wear white overalls that fit tightly around wrists and ankles. They also wear large hats with veils to protect their faces and keep cool. Heavy gloves are worn to protect the hands, and boots with thick soles are worn to prevent slipping, since sudden motions startle honeybees. Beekeepers use smokers, which release smoke to calm the honeybees. Give each child a copy of the *Be a Beekeeper* worksheet (page 31). Have students draw themselves as beekeepers and write about the equipment beekeepers use.

Sweet Bee

Your classroom will be abuzz when students make these candy bees. Give each student two butterscotch candies. Have him open one candy and cut wing shapes from the cellophane wrapper. This candy may be eaten. Untwist and tape down the wrapper edges on the remaining piece of candy. Have him use a black permanent marker to draw details on the wrapped candy to resemble a bee. Attach the wings with clear tape.

Helping Flowers Grow

Children can pretend to be busy bees by pollinating handmade flowers! Explain that honeybees collect pollen, a yellow powder on flowers, to use as food. When a bee lands on a flower, the sticky pollen attaches to the hairs on its legs. When the honeybee alights on another flower and brushes its legs, pollen drops onto the flower, pollinating it and enabling it to grow. Divide students into small groups. Let each group copy, color, and cut out the honeybee pattern (page 32). Attach six black pipe cleaner pieces under the pattern to represent the legs. Have each child draw and cut out a large flower shape from colored paper. Fill a small bottle cap with salt and place it in the center of each flower to represent the pollen. Each student can fly the honeybee pattern over the flower, then land and dip the feet into the salt to gather pollen. Then, let students land the honeybees on other flowers and gently rub the honeybee's legs together, leaving some pollen on the flower. Use the completed honeybees to decorate the *Honeycomb Hives* (page 28) by attaching bees to the edges of the "comb."

A Taste of Honey

Let students taste something sweet—honey! Because honeybees gather nectar from different kinds of flowers, there are many honey flavors. Provide spoons, crackers, or apple slices for students to use to sample types of honey. Try offering one light-colored honey (clover, orange-blossom), one dark-colored honey (buckwheat), and one exotic honey (sourwood, sunflower). Pour the honey into honey bears or squeeze bottles to make it easier for students to sample.

Be a Beekeeper

Hat and Veil

Name_____

Bee Smoker

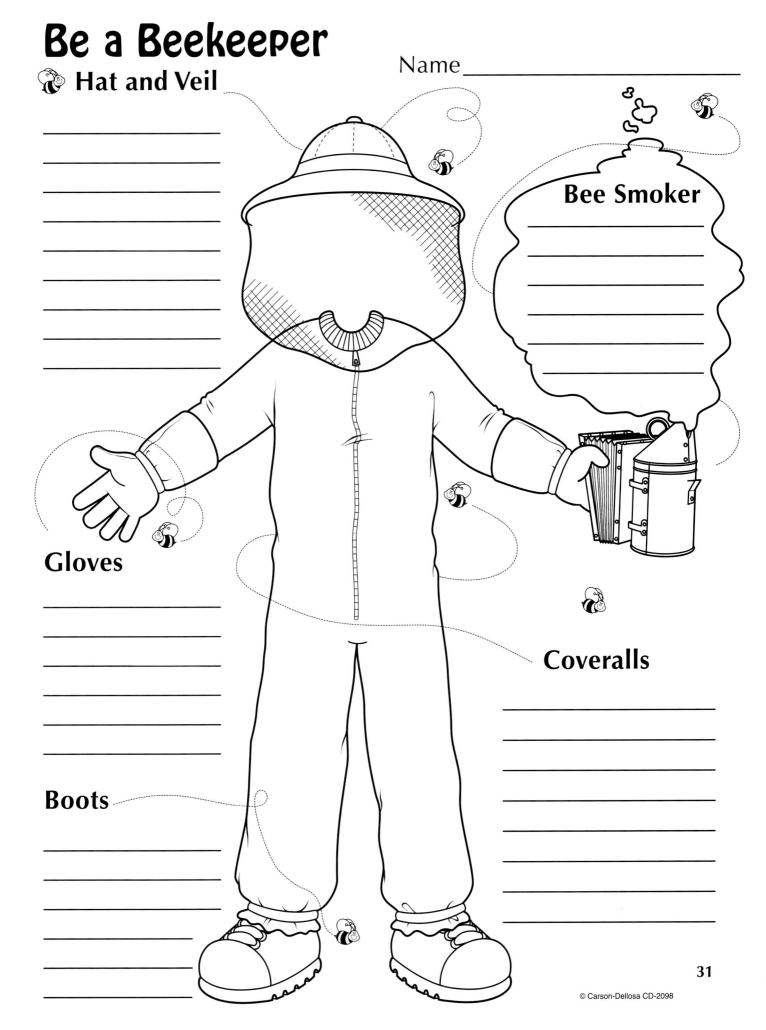

Gloves

Coveralls

Boots

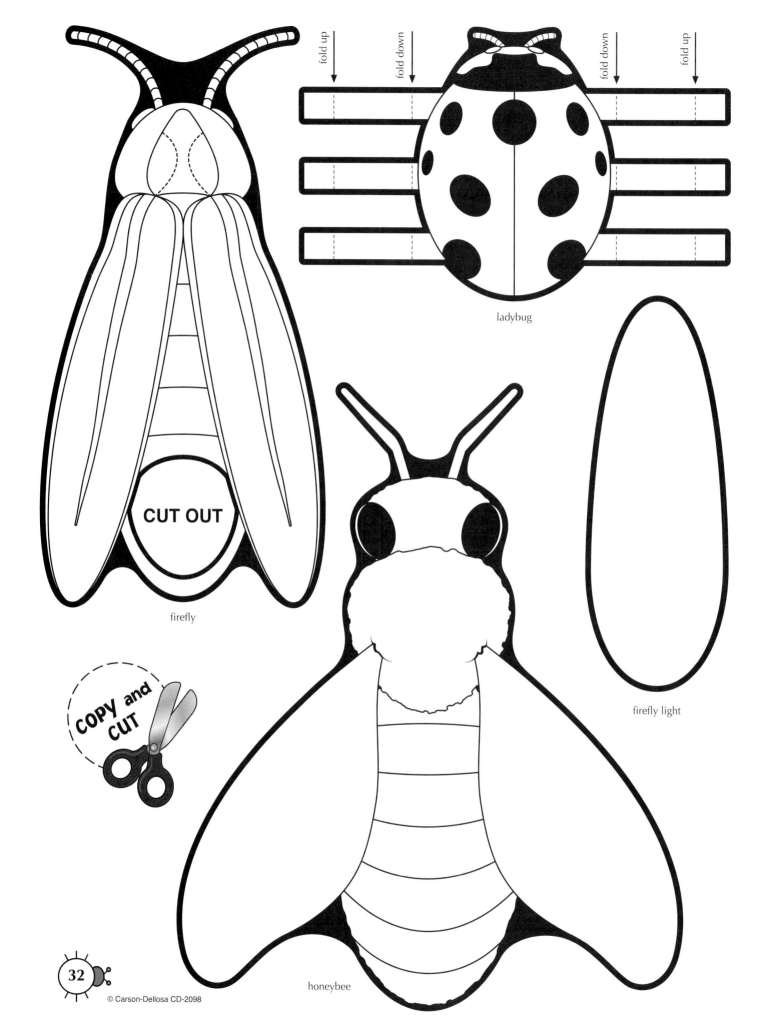

ladybug

fold up   fold down   fold down   fold up

CUT OUT

firefly

firefly light

COPY and CUT

honeybee

moth

butterfly

33

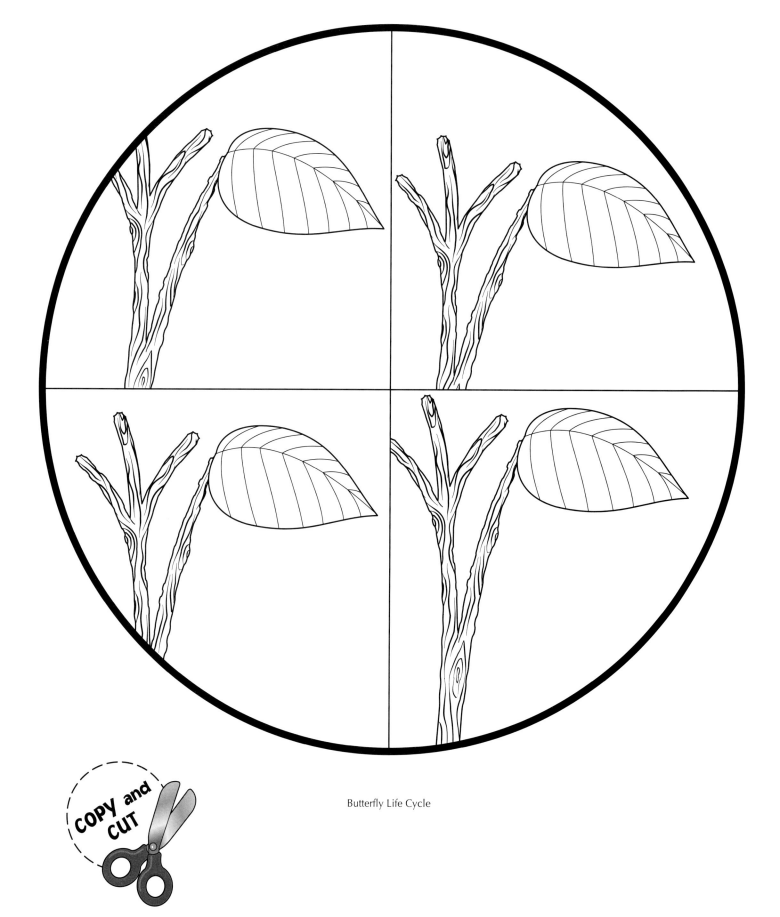

Butterfly Life Cycle

COPY and CUT

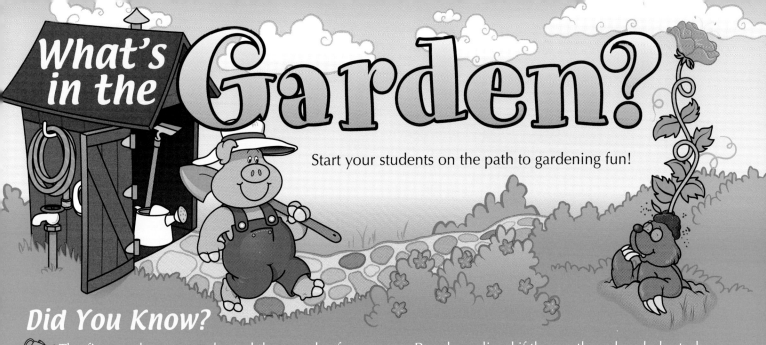

What's in the Garden?

Start your students on the path to gardening fun!

Did You Know?

The first gardens were planted thousands of years ago. People realized if they gathered and planted seeds in one place, they would not have to search large areas for food.

Early civilizations grew ribwort and nettle, plants now considered weeds.

Literature Selections

Alison's Zinnia by Anita Lobel: HarperCollins Publishers, 1990. (Picture book, 32 pg.) Beautiful paintings introduce readers to a variety of flowers in an alphabet book format.

Flower Garden by Eve Bunting: Harcourt Brace, 1999. (Picture book, 32 pg.) A little girl and her father buy flowering plants which they use to create a window box garden.

Garden by Robert Maass: Henry Holt and Company, Inc., 1998. (Picture book, 32 pg.) Stunning photographs depict the colors found in a variety of gardens.

Garden of Happiness by Erika Tamar: Harcourt Brace, 1996. (Picture book, 40 pg.) Marisol and her neighbors plant vegetables and flowers in the city.

How a Seed Grows by Helene J. Jordan: HarperCollins Publishers, 1992. (Picture book, 32 pg.) Presents a clear explanation of how seeds grow into plants.

How Are You Peeling? Foods with Moods by Saxton Freymann and Joost Elffers: Arthur A. Levine, 1999. (Picture book, 48 pg.) Color photographs of fruits and vegetables that show a remarkable range of emotions.

The Ugly Vegetables by Grace Lin: Charlesbridge Publishing, 1999. (Picture book, 32 pg.) As her neighbors' gardens bloom with flowers, a little girl sees only Chinese vegetables in her own. When her mother shares a soup made with the vegetables, everyone appreciates their unusual garden.

Original Flowerpot Art

Add a touch of springtime to your classroom with decorated flowerpots. Supply children with sponges or brushes, acrylic paints, and small clay pots to paint. When the paint dries, fill the pots with soil and let students plant zinnia, marigold, or other seeds that grow well in containers. When the flowers bloom, arrange them on a tabletop to create a colorful indoor garden.

"Handy" Plant Parts

Students can illustrate each part of a plant with their own hands! Trace and cut two hand shapes from brown paper to represent roots, two green hand shapes for leaves, and four colorful hand shapes for flowers. Cut a long strip of green paper for the stem. Attach the roots to the bottom of the stem and the leaves to the sides. Attach a small yellow circle to the top of the stem, then attach four colorful hand shapes around the circle to create a flower. Discuss the function of each part. Roots carry water and minerals from the soil to the plant and also anchor the plant in the ground. The stem carries water and minerals from the roots to the leaves and flowers. It also holds the leaves and flowers upright to expose them to sunlight. Leaves use sunlight to make food for the plant. Flowers produce seeds which may grow into new plants. If possible, provide a few small flowering plants for students to examine in small groups.

Look What's Inside

A close look at the inside of a lima bean reveals a miniature plant! Students can use magnifying glasses to study the tiny leaves, stem, and root inside the bean. Soak dried lima beans in water overnight. Give each child a bean and instruct him to carefully remove the outer covering, or seed coat, which protects the inside of the bean until it sprouts. Have students use their fingers to gently split the beans in half. The tiny leaf and stem on one half of the bean will become the stem and leaves of the plant. The other half contains another tiny stem that will become the roots of the plant. The surrounding area is food that nourishes the seedling. Have each student fold a piece of paper in half and draw a bean shape along the fold. Cut out the shape without cutting the fold. Have students open the bean shapes and draw and label the parts of the bean.

food
root
food
stem
leaves

Watch Our Garden Grow!

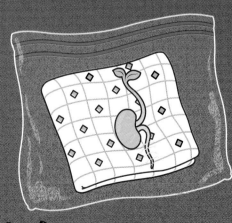

View an underground world by germinating dried lima beans in clear plastic bags. Soak dried lima beans in water overnight to loosen the seed coats and encourage sprouting. Give each child a resealable plastic bag, a moistened paper towel, and a lima bean. Instruct students to place the paper towel inside the bag, then place the lima bean between the bag and the paper towel. Seal the bags, label each with a student's name, and place on a sunny windowsill or staple to a bulletin board exposed to sunlight. Check the beans daily to keep the paper towels moist. Students can draw and describe the changes taking place in a journal. After several weeks, transplant the sprouted seeds into clay pots.

What a Plant Needs

Your students can "write the book" on growing plants! Give each child a sheet of white paper and have him fold it horizontally, then vertically. Instruct students to cut away the folded edges, then stack the pages and turn the booklet horizontally. Staple the pages together along the left-hand side. Have students cut the top three pages in half from top to bottom, leaving the last page full size. On the first page, have each student write the phrase *A plant needs* and draw a plant on the right side of the last page. Then, write and illustrate a sun on the first page, a watering can and sun on the second page, and finally a sun, watering can, and soil on the left side of last page. Explain that plants need three things to flourish—sun, water, and soil. Plants obtain water and nutrients from soil and energy from the sun. Use the booklet to help students remember how to care for classroom plants.

Ready, Set, Grow!

Budding botanists can actually become growing plants! Discuss how seeds need light and water to grow. Turn off the lights and have students pretend to be seeds underground by squatting down with their arms wrapped around their knees. Play a tape recording of rain or tap lightly on a desktop and ask students to pretend to grow a little. Then, turn on the lights and tell the students the sun is shining and they can grow a bit more. Have them continue growing little by little, extending their arms upward until they are as tall as can be.

Getting to the Root of Plants

Observe water traveling up the root of a plant with this experiment. Give each small group of students an 8-ounce plastic cup containing 6 ounces of water. Have each group add ten drops of red food coloring to the water and mix. Give each group a fresh carrot with leaves on top and the bottom tip recently removed. Have students stand the carrots in the cup and place on a sunny windowsill for at least two hours. Then, cut each carrot in half, and each section lengthwise. Use magnifying glasses to see how the tinted water traveled through the carrot. Explain that the edible part of a carrot is its taproot—a primary root that grows vertically downward and gives off small lateral roots.

Bring the Garden Inside

Create a classroom container garden to show off students' green thumbs! Choose easy-to-grow seeds, such as beans, radishes, or zinnias. Create drainage holes in flowerpots, coffee cans, or milk cartons and fill with potting soil. Assign the care of plants to groups of students. Create plant markers by having each student cut out 2 squares of paper. On one square, glue seeds and draw and label a picture of the appropriate plant. On the other square, write growing instructions. Glue the papers back-to-back on a craft stick. As the garden grows, have students write in journals about the changes they see. Have children enclose pressed flowers or leaves from the garden plants in their journals. Conclude the activity by giving each student a Green Thumb Award (page 45).

Beans

COFFEE

Every Gardener's Friend

Ladybugs are truly a gardener's best friend because they eat pests that can damage plants. Some gardeners use ladybugs rather than pesticide. Pay tribute to these hard-working insects by creating garden decorations in their honor. Have each student find a small, smooth stone and wash and dry it. Paint the stone with red acrylic paint. When dry, use a black permanent marker to add dots to resemble a ladybug. Place the ladybugs in plant containers as decorations and reminders of the garden-friendly ladybug.

Garden Foes

Garden Friends or Foes?

Garden Friends

Who goes there—friend or foe? Students will know the difference between garden friends and foes after making these booklets. Have students research which animals and insects are "beneficials" (those that pollinate plants or feed on pests) and which are "pests" (those that feed on leaves, roots, or flowers). Have children include animal or insect names, pictures, explanations about what they do in the garden, and symbols for "friend" or "foe."

slugs
aphids
ants
potato beetles
grasshoppers
caterpillars

ladybugs
praying mantises
lacewings
spiders
bees
fireflies
toads
bats

Tool Aprons

Place garden tools at your students' fingertips! Make gardening aprons by cutting a 12" x 8" piece of poster board for each student. Provide colored paper for students to cut into pocket shapes. Glue them on the poster board, leaving the tops unglued. Decorate the apron and pockets with garden pictures. Make a tie closure by gluing a long length of wide, flat ribbon across the top of the apron. Have students color and cut out copies of the weeder and trowel patterns (pages 42-43). Make garden gloves by having children trace, color, and cut out hand shapes. Design seed packets on small rectangles of paper to slip into the pockets. Students can wear their garden aprons when tending classroom plants.

Take a Walk through the Garden

Students can design and illustrate lovely gardens that are perfect for leisurely strolls. Have each student draw and color an overhead view of a garden plot containing various flowers and vegetables. Let students add an entrance to the garden and then use this as a starting point for a written description of the garden sights, sounds, and smells. Instruct students to write sentences that weave between the plots, creating a walking path through the garden.

Tool Booklets

Have students make garden tool booklets to help them learn the uses of each tool. Make a copy of the garden tools (pages 42-43) for each student. Have children color and cut out the tools and write along the handle how each is used. Punch holes in the handles and tie together with yarn. Students can hang the tools on their aprons or put them in an apron pocket.

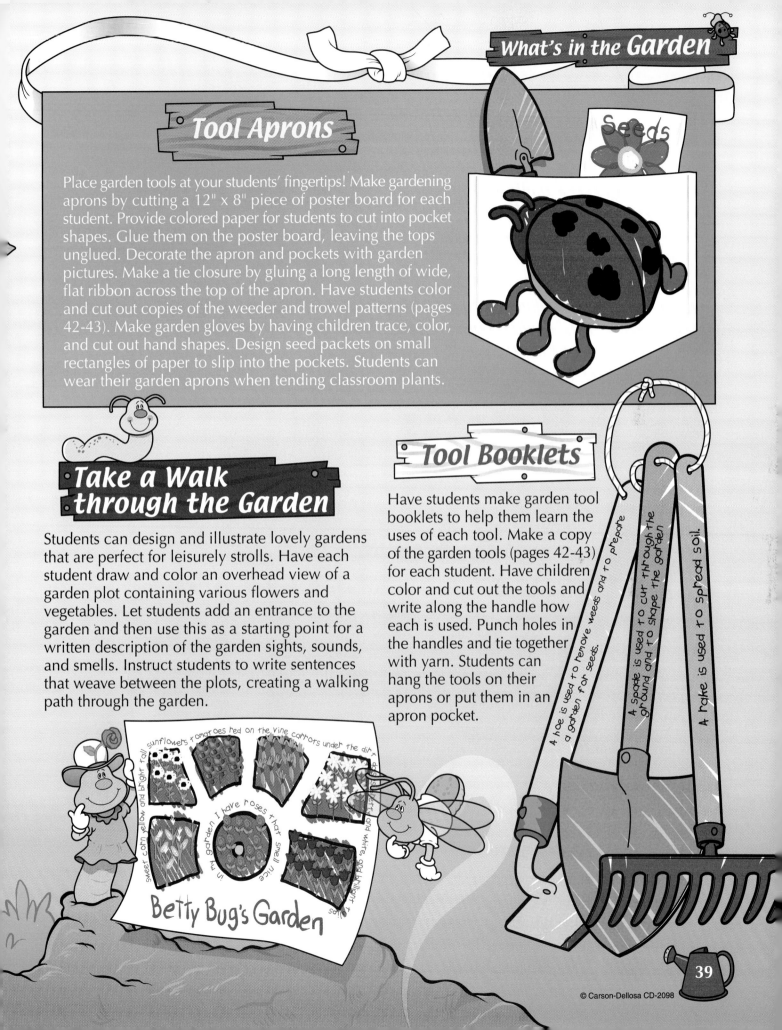

Betty Bug's Garden

Handsome Garden T-shirts

These t-shirts are perfect for classroom gardening. Have students bring in plain white t-shirts. Let children paint their hands with fabric paint, then press them on the shirts. Use paintbrushes to add stems and leaves to the handprint flowers.

Cheerful Sunflowers

Brighten your classroom with sunflowers. Give each student a white paper plate and have him color the outside rim yellow. Draw and cut out petal shapes from the yellow section. Have students color the center of the plate brown and glue sunflower seeds to the center. Cut a tall stem from heavy green paper. Cut leaves from copies of the leaf pattern (page 45) made on green paper. Explain that sunflowers contain edible seeds and provide shelled seeds for students to sample.

Just Add Water

Sprinkle joy in your classroom with these 3-dimensional watering cans.

1. Decorate a strip of 11" x 6" paper; roll into a tube and staple closed. Cut and glue on a circle large enough to make the bottom of the can.

2. Make a spout by rolling an 8" x 5" strip of paper in a tube and stapling closed. Cut and glue on a circle slightly larger than the tube. Use a pencil to punch several tiny holes in the circle.

3. Make an angled cut in the opposite end of the spout and glue this end to the side of the can.

4. Use a pencil to make two holes at the top of the can and insert a pipe cleaner handle. Place blue pipe cleaners in the water spout holes.

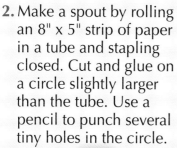

40

Daffodils

Welcome spring with vases of handmade daffodils, tulips, and zinnias! Give each child a copy of the daffodil base pattern (page 45) to trace onto yellow poster board and cut out. Provide small yellow paper cups and instruct students to cut slits around the outside rims. Glue the bottom of the cup to the center of the daffodil base. Cut a stem and long leaves from green poster board and attach to the daffodil.

Tulips

Give each child a section cut from a cardboard egg carton. Have students scallop the edges with scissors and then paint them—inside and out. When dry, have each student poke a hole in the center of a tulip and insert a green pipe cleaner. Slide a yellow bead onto the tip of the pipe cleaner (inside the tulip). Slide a green bead to the base of the flower to help the blossom stand upright.

Vase

Cut paper to fit around a large cardboard tube. Have students decorate the paper with markers and wrap it around the outside of the tube, gluing to secure. For the vase bottom, cut a 4" circle from paper and cut out a hole the size of the cardboard tube. Slide the paper base onto the bottom of the vase. Allow students to arrange their handmade flowers in the vases.

Zinnias

Cut a large, medium, and small circle from a single color of paper. Fringe the circles by cutting slits around the edges of each one and then curling them with a pencil. Layer the circles with the largest one on the bottom. Put several thin strips of yellow paper in the center of the smallest circle. Place a paper fastener through the center of the stack to attach the pieces. Cut a stem for each flower from green construction paper. Cut leaves from construction paper or use green paper copies of the leaf pattern (page 45).

41

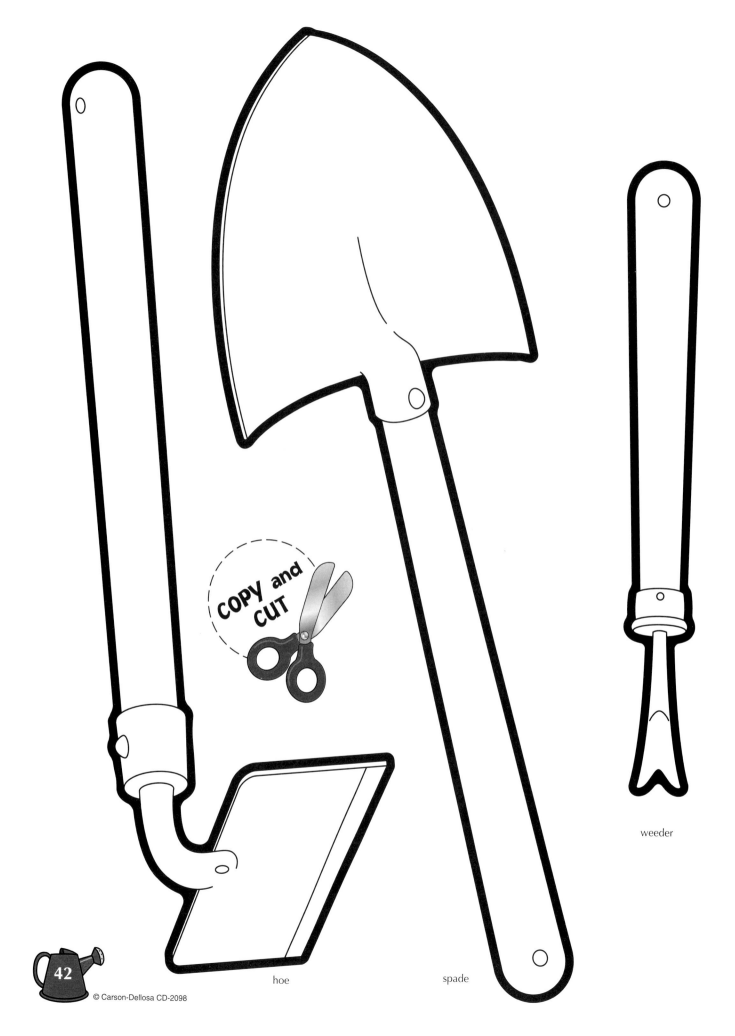

COPY and CUT

weeder

hoe

spade

trowel

rake

cultivator

43

tulip
(use with bulletin board idea pg. 15)

daisy
(use with bulletin board idea pg. 15)

COPY and CUT

44

© Carson-Dellosa CD-2098

sunflower
(use with bulletin board ideas pgs. 15 and 16)

daffodil base

leaf

Use a green ink pad for thumb prints.

Green Thumb Award

Presented to:

Certified Thumb Print

45

Delightful, Delicious Berries!

Make the most of May by exposing your students to the delectable fruits harvested this month—strawberries and blueberries! They inspire poetry, art, and they taste good!

Did You Know?

- A single strawberry has over 200 seeds and is the only fruit with its seeds on the outside.
- The Wampanoag Indians taught the settlers at Plymouth to gather and dry native blueberries.
- Strawberries were named because of the way the runners *strew* or spread along the ground.
- Many historians believe a blueberry and corn pudding was served at the first Thanksgiving feast.

Sweet Strawberries

by Phyllis Reynolds Naylor: Atheneum, 1999. (Illustrated storybook, 40 pg.) An amusing tale of faults, patience, forgiveness, and sweet strawberries.

The Big Hungry Bear

by Audrey Wood: Childs Play, 1990. (Illustrated storybook, 32 pg.) The reader plays the role of narrator in this tale about a little mouse, a red ripe strawberry, and a big hungry bear.

Jamberry

by Bruce Degen: HarperCollins, 1990. (Illustrated storybook, 32 pg.) A boy and a bear frolic in *Berryland* where they encounter raspberry rabbits and topple their canoeberry with blueberries. Silly rhymes and a musical beat make it a good read-aloud book.

Blueberry Shoe

by Ann Dixon: Alaska Northwest Books, 1999. (Illustrated storybook, 32 pg.) A baby's shoe lost in a blueberry patch acquires a variety of uses by a fox, a vole, and a bear until the next summer when the family returns and makes a startling discovery.

"Berry" Beautiful Bulletin Board

Create a fruity bulletin board to inform students about the different growing habits of these tasty berries. Explain that strawberries grow on low-growing, spreading plants and blueberries grow on bushes that can be as high as 12 feet. Copy the strawberry and blueberry patterns (page 49) for children to color. Add dimension to the strawberries by gluing on watermelon seeds. To enhance the blueberries, glue pieces of tissue paper to resemble the blossom end or *calyx* (KAY•licks). Create a colorful border with these student-made berries. Create a berry garden by drawing the canes and leaves of a blueberry bush, then let students place the tips of their fingers in blue tempera paint and fill the bush with blueberries. Draw strawberry plants beside the blueberry bush and let students place their thumbs in red tempera paint to form the strawberries. Use fine-point markers to add detail to the berries.

46

Strawberry Journals

Grow a classroom strawberry plant near a sunny window. Start the plant in a "hen and chick" pot which allows the plant to send off runners and create "daughter" plants. Let students take care of the plant by watering it weekly, feeding it with a liquid fertilizer either monthly or weekly, turning the pot 1/4 turn each day to keep the growth uniform, and by making sure that the runners take root in soil. Let each student keep an illustrated and written journal of the plant's growth. Use the strawberry pattern (page 49) to make shaped journals. Let each student color the pattern as a cover and then duplicate pages on white paper for the inside pages. As you watch the plant grow, blossom, and form fruit, you might plan a trip to a local strawberry field where children can pick. Call your local agricultural extension office to help find a field. Back in class, have students write about their field trip experiences in their strawberry journals.

Share these tips with your berry pickers:
- Stay in the pathways and be careful not to step on plants.
- Look under the leaves for berries.
- Handle the berries gently.
- Pick all fully ripe fruit, both large and small.
- Don't pile the berries too high.
- Wash berries before eating.

Blueberry Star

The Wampanoag Indians called blueberries *Star Berries* because of the perfect five-pointed star on the calyx, or blossom end, of each berry. Students can make a 3-dimensional blueberry that will highlight this five-pointed star. Have each student cut out one blue and one purple circle. Draw 5 lines (see diagram) on the blue circle and cut through these lines. Push back the flaps. Glue the blue circle over the purple circle. Have students write words describing blueberries inside the calyx. If desired, inspire them with Robert Frost's description of blueberries: "The blue's but a mist from the breath of the wind."

Pretty Berry Baskets

Recycle used fruit baskets to create lovely spring baskets! Your local grocer will likely let you have these at minimal or no cost. Wash and clean the baskets. Fold 30" strips of crepe paper, ribbon, or fabric strips lengthwise. Weave the material in and out of the basket. Attach a bow with a twist tie or weave the top row with a separate piece of material, leaving an 8" section at the beginning and end to tie into a bow. Braid three colors of pipe cleaner together and attach to either side of the basket for a handle. For a special effect, catch short pieces of the weaving material into the pipe cleaners as they are braided. Let children fill their baskets with paper flowers or take the class on a walk to find signs of spring to place in their baskets.

47

Berry Swirl Treat

The highlight of your berry study can be this delicious cold soup. Let each student sample the soup in class and then write the recipe on a pre-lined copy of a berry pattern (page 49) to take home and share.

Place 1 cup blueberries in a blender and process until smooth. Strain to remove skins. Add 1/2 cup buttermilk and 1/2 cup plain yogurt and mix well. Refrigerate until chilled.

Blend 1 cup strawberries in a blender and process until smooth. Stir in 1/2 cup vanilla yogurt and refrigerate until chilled.

To serve the soup, divide blueberry mixture into four bowls. Add one quarter of the strawberry mixture to one side of the blueberry mixture in each bowl. Let students use a clean craft stick to swirl the mixtures together.

Strawberry Blueberry Jam

Children will like learning how jam is made and having their own small jar of jam to take home. Let each student design a paper label to wrap around her jar. Attach labels after the jars have been filled.

Directions

1. Have an adult rinse a small jar and lid with boiling water for each student.
2. Stem and slice 1 1/2 pints of strawberries and 1 pint of blueberries. Crush berries thoroughly, one layer at a time. Place 1 1/2 cups strawberries in a large bowl. Crush blueberries one layer at a time. Put 1 cup of blueberries in bowl with strawberries. Stir in 4 1/2 cups sugar. Let stand 10 minutes; stirring occasionally.
3. Mix 3/4 cup of water and a 1 3/4-ounce box of pectin in a small saucepan. Bring mixture to a boil, stirring constantly. Continue boiling and stirring for 1 minute. Stir pectin mixture into fruit mixture. Stir constantly for 3 minutes to dissolve sugar.
4. Fill containers quickly to within 1/2" of tops and cover with lids. Let stand at room temperature 24 hours. Store jam in refrigerator up to 3 weeks. Fills 12 1/2-cup containers.

Shortcake for All!

Enjoy the reward of a trip to the fields by serving a special shortcake snack.

- 2 quarts fresh berries
- 3/4 cup sugar
- 2 prepared pound cake loaves
- 1 16-ounce container whipped topping

Wash and slice the berries and sprinkle with sugar. Mash slightly for extra juice. Cut the cakes into 7 slices each and then cut lengthwise to total 14 slices per cake. For each serving, place a slice of cake in a bowl, cover it with berries, and top with whipped topping. Makes 28 servings.

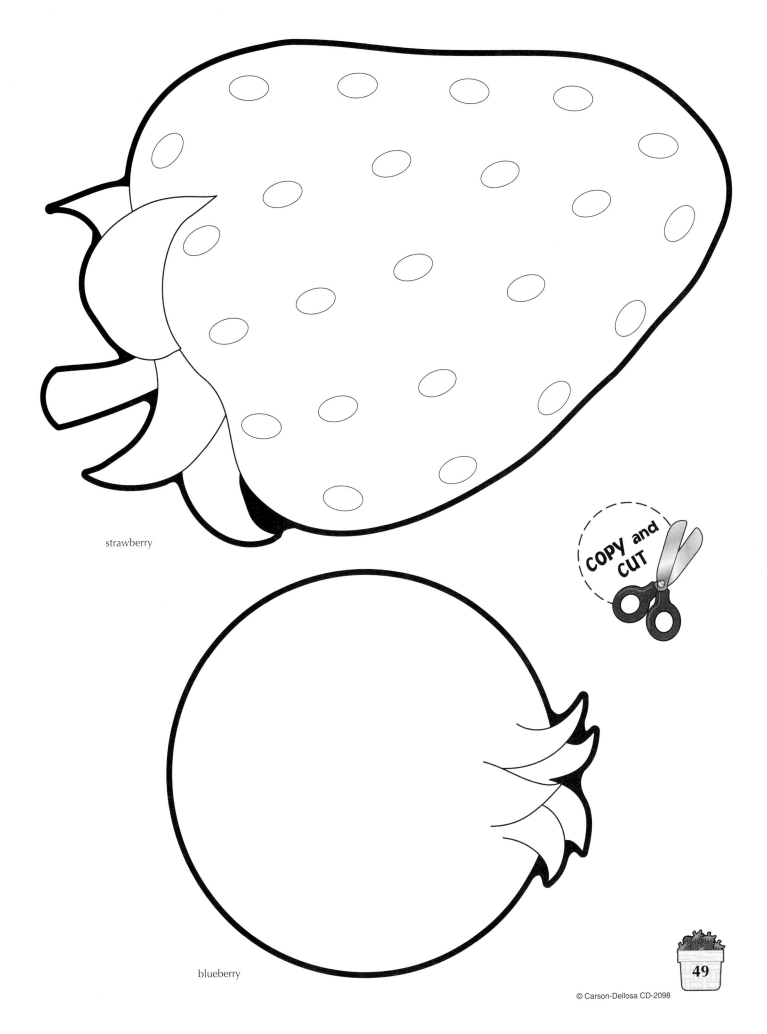

strawberry

COPY and CUT

blueberry

Mother's Day — A Tribute to Moms

People all over the world have honored mothers for centuries for their nurturing, caring, and loving ways. Help students say "thanks" to their mothers on Mother's Day, the second Sunday in May, with these easy and fun ideas.

Did You Know?

- In 17th century England, Mothering Sunday was celebrated on the fourth Sunday during Lent. Sons and daughters traveled home to visit their mothers and bring them sweets and other gifts.
- In 1872, Julia Ward Howe, the writer of the song *Battle Hymn of the Republic*, tried to establish a Mother's day. It became official in 1914 when Anna Jarvis petitioned the government to proclaim a national Mother's Day.
- *Mother* sounds similar in many languages— *mutter* (MUHT•ter) in German, *mère* (MARE) in French, and *madre* (MAH•dray) in Italian and Spanish.

Literature Selections

A Gift for Mama by Esther Hautzig: Puffin, 1997. (Illustrated storybook, 64 pg.) Tired of making presents for various occasions, Sara decides to do something different for this Mother's Day.

No Time for Mother's Day by Laurie Halse Anderson: Albert Whitman & Co., 1999. (Picture book, 32 pg.) Seeing how busy her mother is, Charity decides on the best gift for her on Mother's Day.

The Mother's Day Mice by Eve Bunting: Houghton Mifflin Co., 1986. (Picture book, 32 pg.) Three little mice search for the perfect gift for their mother for Mother's Day.

Cute as a Button Necklace

Make mom feel special when she wears this simple handmade necklace. Provide an assortment of buttons (with at least two holes) and black or white heavy-duty thread. Encourage students to pick seven buttons that are similar in color and one larger button or bead. Give each child a length of thread 18"-20" and have her thread the seven buttons onto the thread, coming up from the bottom of each button and going back down the other hole, so the buttons lay flat against the thread. Help the children space the buttons 1" apart along the front of the necklace. Tie a loop in one end of the thread and tie the larger button to the other end. Put this button through the loop to clasp the necklace.

Giving cards on Mother's Day has become a popular tradition. Help students personalize Mother's Day cards and create envelopes in *Put Your Stamp On It!* (below). Fold a 7" x 11" piece of construction paper in half. Have students decorate the cards and then write the *My Mom...* poem (left) inside. Remind children to keep their own moms in mind when completing the lines. (A student may write a poem about an important female in her life by replacing "My mom" with "My grandma," for example.)

My mom is
My mom likes
My mom knows
My mom says, "   "
My mom can
My mom wishes
My mom loves
My mom is (repeat 1st line)

My Mom
My mom is the best
My mom likes quilting
My mom knows how to play the guitar
My mom says, "be a share girl"
My mom can cook
My mom wishes that I am happy
My mom loves me
My mom is the best

Put Your Stamp On It!

In 1934, a special Mother's Day stamp was issued featuring the famous painting, *Whistler's Mother*; along with carnations, the symbol of Mother's Day; and the words, "In memory and in honor of the mothers of America." Let students design their own Mother's Day stamps on homemade envelopes. **1.** To make an envelope, trace a greeting card from *Greetings* (above) in the middle of an 11" x 17" piece of white paper, then draw triangles along each edge of the traced card. **2.** Cut out the shape, fold each triangle in along the lines, and tape the bottom and two side triangles together in the middle. Have each student design a Mother's Day stamp in the upper right corner of his envelope and address the envelope to his mother. Let each child place his card inside his envelope and seal it with a sticker or tape.

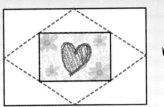

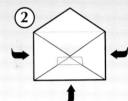

Motherly Traditions

Children can learn maternal history by interviewing their mothers about motherhood. A child can ask what lullabies, foods, hobbies, games, or sayings his mother first learned from her mother. Have children write reports on their mothers' traditions and share them with the class. If desired, display the completed reports on a bulletin board titled *From My Grandmother to My Mother, to Me!*

51

Fragrant Flowers

Carnations are the official symbol of Mother's Day because they were Anna Jarvis' mother's favorite flower. In the language of flowers, carnations represent sweetness, purity, and endurance. Help children make fragrant carnations for their mothers. **1.** Stack five layers of white or pink tissue paper (5" x 9") on top of each other and accordion fold. (To tint the edge of the petals, color with a crayon or marker along the long edges of each tissue before stacking and folding.) **2.** Slightly round each end of the folded tissues with scissors **3.** Wrap the end of a green pipe cleaner around the middle of the tissues. Twist tightly to secure. Carefully pull apart and puff up the layers to form petals. Use an eye-dropper to add cinnamon or other scented oil to the flower and give to mom!

Stained Glass Candle Holder

Help mom relax on her special day with a glowing candle holder. Let each student tear several colors of tissue paper into small pieces. Use a watered-down white glue solution and a small paintbrush to smooth the tissue paper pieces onto the outer surface of a clean, dry, baby food jar. Layer the tissue to cover the jar completely with a colorful pattern. When the glue is dry, place a tea light inside the jar. When mom lights the tea light, the colored tissue paper will glow like stained glass!

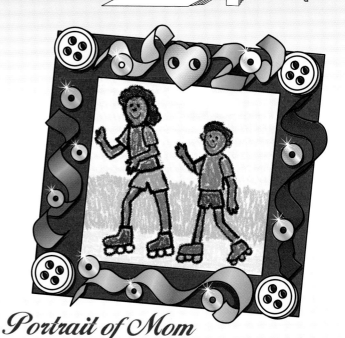

Portrait of Mom

Mother and child in a decorative frame will be treasured by Mom. Have each child illustrate himself doing something with his mother. Create frames by cutting poster board 2" bigger on all sides than the pictures. Cut out an area in the center of each poster board piece slightly smaller than the picture. Decorate the frame with sequins, ribbon, etc. Tape the pictures to the backs of the poster board frames and attach magnetic tape. Hang the pictures on a Mother's Day wall for students to enjoy before taking home for Mother's Day.

Handy Flower Pot

Give mom a hand for all she does! Let each child "plant" handprint flowers in a hand-decorated pot. Provide a clay pot for each child. Let students glue several large buttons randomly around them. Then, glue smaller buttons around each big button to make petals. Use green acrylic paint for the stems and leaves. Glue plastic foam (available at craft stores) inside the pot and cover with green tissue paper. Paint craft sticks green and glue several together to make long stems. Cut out green leaves from construction paper and glue to the stems. Help each child press his hand in a shallow pan of finger paint and make several prints on white poster board. Let the prints dry, cut them out, and glue one to the end of each craft stick stem. Poke the stems into the plastic foam. Add a gift tag that reads, "Mom, you deserve a hand!"

Mom,
you deserve
a hand!

Sweet Treats for Mom

Mom can enjoy this easy-to-make treat any time! In a bowl, mix 1 cup sugar, $^1/_2$ cup unsweetened cocoa, 1 cup powdered milk, $^1/_4$ cup instant coffee and $^1/_2$ teaspoon cinnamon. Let each student measure out 2 tablespoons of mix into a small plastic bag and tie with a ribbon. Attach a gift tag with the directions, "Add 1 cup hot water and stir." The recipe makes about 12 2-tablespoon servings. Present mix to mom along with a chocolate spoon (right) for yummy stirring.

Chocolate Spoons

Coffee, cocoa, or a mocha drink, like *Sweet Treats for Mom* (left) can be that much better when stirred with a chocolate spoon. Melt chocolate chips in a microwave, then dip the bowl of a plastic spoon into the chocolate. Place the spoon on a sheet of wax paper and place in the freezer. When the chocolate hardens, wrap the bowl of the spoon in plastic wrap and tie with ribbon.

Asian Pacific American Heritage Month

Did You Know?

- President George Bush signed a law in 1992 to proclaim May as Asian Pacific American Heritage Month.
- Chinese workers are primarily responsible for the building of the Central Pacific Railroad—America's first transcontinental railway system.
- Many popular toys and games originated in Asian Pacific countries. For example, the yo-yo was originally a Filipino weapon, Parcheesi is an Indian game, and the kite originated in China.

This annual, month-long celebration is meant to promote awareness of the diversity within the Asian Pacific American culture and recognize the contributions of Asian Pacific Americans.

Literature Selections

Angel Child, Dragon Child by Michele Surat Surat: Scholastic Trade, 1989. (Storybook, 40 pg.) A homesick Vietnamese girl adjusts to life in the United States.

Dumpling Soup by Jama Kim Ratiigan: Little Brown & Co., 1998. (Picture book, 32 pg.) An Asian Pacific American girl living in Hawaii learns her family's tradition of making dumplings.

Halmoni and the Picnic by Sook Nyul Choi: Houghton Mifflin Co., 1993. (Storybook, 31 pg.) A Korean-American girl helps her grandmother get used to living in America and teaches her classmates about her Korean heritage.

Countries of Origin

The term *Asian Pacific* refers to a wide range of countries, from India to Fiji, whose languages, cultures, and histories are immensely diverse. Show students what a large area of the world these countries cover. Have students find each country and island listed. Based on their locations, ask students to guess on which coast in North America did most early Asian Pacific American immigrants arrive (this may best be done on a globe). Ask students if they think people in one country speak the same language, eat the same food, etc., as people in another, and have them explain their answers.

China	Laos
India	Thailand
Myanmar	Malaysia
Cambodia	Singapore
Japan	Pakistan
Korea	Sri Lanka
Vietnam	Polynesia
Philippines	Micronesia
Bangladesh	Melanesia
Indonesia	Hawaii

Pacific Ocean

Tea Time

A legend says that tea was invented in China thousands of years ago when tea leaves accidentally blew into a pot of boiling water and an emperor drank the water and liked it. Tea is grown in most Asian countries and is enjoyed all over the world. Americans have even adopted their own way to drink tea…iced! Have a tea party with students and let them sample several types of tea including green tea, iced tea, and various black teas and experiment with adding sugar, milk, and lemon. Also try this spicy Indian tea recipe, Chai tea.

Chai Tea

2 cups milk
6-8 strips lemon or orange zest
2 cups water
1 teaspoon cardamom seeds
2 cinnamon sticks, broken

16 whole cloves
2 tablespoons loose black tea
   (Use *Darjeeling* if possible,
   an Indian tea)
3 tablespoons sugar

Combine ingredients (except tea and sugar) in a saucepan. Bring to a boil, cover and reduce heat to low. Simmer for 15-20 minutes. Add the tea and simmer for 5-10 minutes. Strain the mixture. Add sugar to liquid and serve hot. Makes 8 small servings.

Amazing Achievers

Many Asian Pacific Americans are famous for their individual achievements. Have students report on the lives and contributions of famous Asian Pacific Americans, including Maya Lin, Amy Tan, Subrahmanyan Chandresekhar, Yo-Yo Ma, Tiger Woods, Kristi Yamaguchi, and I.M. Pei. Ask students to draw and cut out objects that represent the contribution of their famous person, then write their reports on the cut-outs. For example, a report on Yo-Yo Ma may be written on a cut-out of a cello. Have each child read his report to the class, then display the reports on a bulletin board titled *Asian Pacific American Achievers*.

Posies from Paradise

Instead of Asian Pacific immigrants coming to America, America came to them when Hawaii became the fiftieth state in 1959. The majority of its inhabitants are native Hawaiians and people from Japan, China, and the Philippines. Hawaii exports many important crops including pineapples, sugar, and flowers. Make two popular Hawaiian flowers, the Anthurium and the Bird of Paradise.

To make an Anthurium, cut a heart shape with a rounded bottom from red paper. Poke a small hole in the middle, about an inch from the top, and draw curved lines radiating from the hole. Poke a white pipe cleaner through the hole. Attach a green pipe cleaner to the white one at the back for a stem.

To make a Bird of Paradise, cut a long beak shape from green construction paper with a slit at the top (see illustration.) Cut petal shapes from orange and yellow tissue paper, slide into the slit, and tape on the back to secure. Tape the flower to a green pipe cleaner for a stem. Arrange the flowers in containers around the room for a beautiful Hawaiian display.

55

"Sun"sational Summer Books

Summer is a great time to relax with a good book! Share these wonderful stories and fun activities with your students!

Come On, Rain
by Karen Hesse: Scholastic Press, 1999
(Picture book, 32 pg.)

A young girl hopes for rain on a hot day in the city. She enlists her friends to put on bathing suits and wait for the rain. When it does come, their mothers join them for a spirited dance in the much-needed rain.

The rain is like icy fingers tickling me.

Help students picture themselves dancing in the cool rain on a hot summer day. Have each student cut out a bathing suit from fabric or wall paper scraps, glue the fabric to paper, and draw a picture of himself in the bathing suit. Ask students to write sentences describing the rain, or how it feels to be in the rain, on their pictures. Use the imagery in the story as inspiration: *It freckles our feet, glazes our toes, …glistening in our rain skin, …romping and reeling in the moisty green air, …laughing under trinkets of silver rain, The rain has made us new.* Finally, use watercolors to add rain. Let students make streaks and drops of blue and gray paint on their papers, then brush the background with the tinted water. Display the pictures with the title *Come On, Rain!*

Canoe Days
by Gary Paulsen: Bantam Doubleday Dell Publishing Group, Inc., 1999. (Picture book, 32 pg.)

Soft paintings and simple text take the reader on a serene canoe ride on a beautiful summer day. The lake and its inhabitants are quiet but awe-inspiring.

Encourage students to reflect on nature's beauty. In the middle of the story the author describes the water as a "window into the skylake." Look at the illustration of the "skylake" and talk with students about what the author means. Then, let students create their own pictures where the water "becomes part of the sky." Have each student fold a sheet of white construction paper in half lengthwise. Unfold and orient horizontally. The top half of the paper will be the earth and sky and the bottom half will be the water. Use acrylic paints, diluted with water, to paint trees, shrubs, etc., on the top half, and paint a shoreline at the crease. Lightly brush water over the painting to re-wet the paint, being careful not to smear the picture. Fold along the crease and press and rub hard on the back. This will transfer the image to the bottom of the paper, creating the reflection in the lake. Unfold and touch up the picture if necessary.

We Had a Picnic This Sunday Past

by Jacqueline Woodson: Hyperion Books
for Children, 1998. (Picture book, 32 pg.)

A family picnic is described from a young girl's perspective filtered through her grandmother's point of view. Learn the inside scoop about each family member as he or she arrives, and everyone anticipates Cousin Martha's dreaded dried-out apple pie.

Have a class picnic and keep track of who brings what with this memory game. Cover a bulletin board with a picnic table cloth, and let each child draw on a paper plate a picture of what she would bring to the picnic. Have each child staple her completed plate to the "picnic table," introducing herself and telling what she brought. Challenge each child not only to say what she brought, but to name previous children and their picnic items. If children cannot remember what others brought, they can look at the bulletin board for help.

Grandma Summer

by Harley Jessup: Viking, 1999. (Picture book, 32 pg.)

A boy spends a summer with his grandmother in an old family beach house. While determined to be miserable at first, the boy finds a blown-glass float from a fishing net on the beach and discovers its interesting history. He also finds himself having a great time.

Have students comb the beach for treasure by imagining an object they would like to find washed up on shore. Let each student make up an interesting history for that object. Have each child fold a sheet of paper in half horizontally and cut a wave pattern along the bottom edge of the top layer. Draw a picture of the object on the front and color blue waves around it. Unfold the paper, lightly color the inside tan to represent sand, and write a story telling where the object was found, where it came from, how far it traveled, what it was used for, etc. If desired, draw a map similar to the one in the book to accompany the story. Let each student present her object to the class and explain its history.

Hello!
Help me, I'm stuck on a...

go, but I gave the message and map to the coast guard. I kept the bottle as a memento.

57

THE PICNIC

by Ruth Brown: Dutton Children's Books, 1992. (Picture book, 28 pg.)

Stunning illustrations offer a unique perspective of a family's picnic as viewed by underground animals. The humans and their dog seem terrifying from the underground vantage point, but rain soon sends them away and the animals come out and enjoy a picnic of their own.

Children can make their own peek-inside picnic books! Have each student fold white paper in half and orient the fold along the top. Cut a ³/₄" wide strip from the left edge of only the top layer, starting at the top and stopping at the fold. Cut a hole in the middle of the top layer and color an underground scene with rabbits and other animals looking out the hole. Lift the top layer and draw an item found at a picnic on the bottom half of the paper so that part of it can be seen through the hole when the flap is closed. Gather each child's page, add a cover and bind along the left edge. As students read the book, challenge them to identify the items seen through the holes, then lift the flaps to reveal the pictures.

My Life With the Wave

translated and adapted by Catherine Cowen: Lothrop, Lee & Shepard Books, 1997. (Picture book, 32 pg.)

A boy brings a wave home from the beach to live in his house. The wave has many moods, some comforting, some destructive. The boy's parents eventually insist that the wave be returned to the ocean. Don't miss the cat, dog, mouse, whale, and sea horse hidden in almost every illustration.

Let students imagine the sequel to this book! At the end of the story, the boy thinks about bringing home a cloud from his next vacation, believing it would be "soft and cuddly and would never act like a wave." The last illustration hints that he may be in for even more trouble! Have students predict what would happen by matching human emotions to the many forms and actions of a cloud, just as the author did with the wave. Write a variety of emotions, such as *sad, angry, happy, scared*, etc., on index cards and give one to each student. Challenge him to draw a picture that shows how he thinks a cloud would look if it were experiencing that emotion. Provide cotton balls to accent the clouds. Display the pictures and their emotion words with the title *The Many Moods of a Cloud*.

MR. CAREY'S GARDEN
by Jane Cutler: Houghton Mifflin Co., 1996. (Picture book, 32 pg.)

Four neighbors each have a garden that is special, but no one can figure out why Mr. Carey's garden, full of chewed up plants, is so special to him. One hot summer night when no one can sleep, the neighbors discover what makes Mr. Carey's garden so special.

Help students make shimmering snail gardens like Mr. Carey's! Let each child use crayons to draw a garden scene on black paper. Then, coil 7" pieces of yarn over spots of glue on the paper to make snail shells. Glue 1" yarn pieces under each coil for the head or tail. Use silver glitter to form shimmering snail trails behind each snail. Include a silvery moon, sprinkled with glitter. Have each child add details to his garden and then explain why his is also "special."

Touch the Sky Summer
by Jean Van Leeuwen: Dial Books for Young Readers, 1997. (Picture book, 32 pg.)

Realistic oil paintings enhance a boy's description of a favorite summer vacation at his grandparents' lakeside cabin. Swimming, fishing, camping, and hiking are all part of this fondly-remembered family experience.

Share favorite summer memories through words and pictures! Ask each child to write about a favorite summer memory. Encourage students to add dialog and descriptive details to their stories, as the author did in *Touch the Sky Summer*. Then, have each student draw a picture that sums up his story and display the picture on a bulletin board. Let one child at a time read his story and challenge classmates to guess which picture goes with his summer story.

59

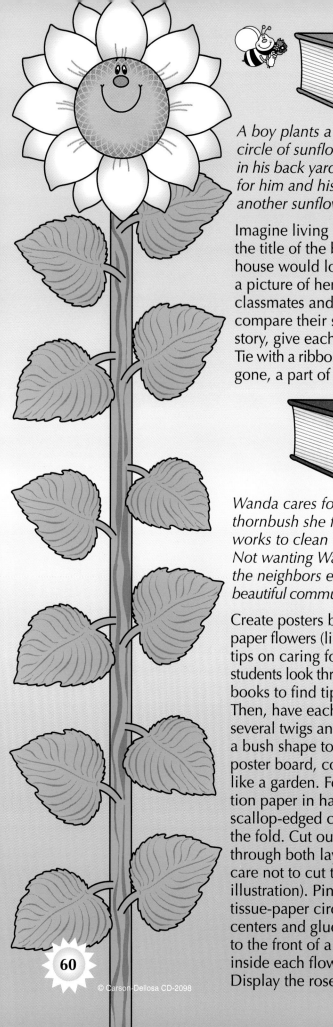

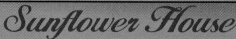

Sunflower House
by Eve Bunting: Harcourt Brace & Co.,
1996. (Picture book, 32 pg.)

*A boy plants a
circle of sunflower seeds
in his back yard. As the flowers grow, they form a fun and beautiful playhouse
for him and his friends. When the flowers die, he gathers the seeds to plant
another sunflower house next year.*

Imagine living in a sunflower house! Before reading the story, tell students
the title of the book and ask them to imagine what they think a sunflower
house would look like. Give each child a sheet of paper and have her draw
a picture of her sunflower house. Let students share their houses with
classmates and display them on a bulletin board. Then, read the story and
compare their sunflower houses to the one in the story. At the end of the
story, give each student a small bag of unshelled sunflower seeds to plant.
Tie with a ribbon and tag with the message: "It's neat to think when something's
gone, a part of it goes on and on." —Eve Bunting from *Sunflower House*.

WANDA'S ROSES
by Pat Brisson: Boyds Mills Press, 1994
(Picture book, 32 pg.)

*Wanda cares for a
thornbush she finds in an abandoned lot, believing it to be a rosebush. She
works to clean up the lot and invites her neighbors to a rose garden party.
Not wanting Wanda to feel badly that her bush has not produced any roses,
the neighbors each bring a rosebush and transform the empty lot into a
beautiful community rose garden.*

Create posters blooming with
paper flowers (like Wanda's) and
tips on caring for roses. Let
students look through gardening
books to find tips for roses.
Then, have each child gather
several twigs and glue them in
a bush shape to a piece of
poster board, colored to look
like a garden. Fold construction paper in half and draw
scallop-edged circles along
the fold. Cut out the circles
through both layers, taking
care not to cut the fold (see
illustration). Pinch several
tissue-paper circles in the
centers and glue each circle
to the front of a cut-out. Write a rose care tip
inside each flower. Glue the roses around the twigs on the poster.
Display the rosebushes to create a pretty and informative rose garden.

Roses need plenty of water and fertilizer.

Keep weeds away from rose bushes.

The Summer My Father Was Ten

by Pat Brisson: Boyds Mills Press, Inc.,
1999 (Picture book, 32 pg.)

RESPECT

Respect is when you look up to someone and think they deserve to be treated nicely.

The boy was not showing respect when he picked a tomato from Mr. Bellavista's garden without permission.

A young girl recalls the story her dad tells her each year when they plant their garden together. The story is about a time when he carelessly ruined a neighbor's garden, but eventually made amends by helping the neighbor grow a new garden the next year.

Examine a story character's character! Before reading the story, post a list of positive character traits (courage, integrity, compassion, respect, etc.) and discuss the meaning of each. When reading the story, refer to the list and have students point out the character traits that the girl's father does and does not exhibit at different times throughout the story. Then, let each child choose a trait to define. Have her write the term at the top of a sheet of paper, write a definition in her own words, and illustrate a scene from the story that either shows the trait or the lack of it. Finish by writing a short sentence that contains the character word and explains the illustration.

An Asian-American girl and her mother plant a backyard garden. The girl watches as her neighbors' gardens bloom with beautiful flowers, while hers grows "ugly" Chinese vegetables. After the mother makes a delicious soup with the vegetables, everyone comes to appreciate these "ugly" plants.

The Ugly Vegetables

by Grace Lin: Charlesbridge Publishing,
1999. (Picture book, 32 pg.)

Flavor your classroom with Chinese vegetable crafts! The last page of the book provides information about each of the vegetables mentioned in the book, including their Chinese characters, pictures, pronunciations, descriptions, and an Ugly Vegetable Soup recipe. If possible, locate the vegetables at an Asian market and make the soup for the children to taste after reading the book. Then, let the students make garden tags for the vegetables. Give each child a 4" x 4" square of white poster board and a craft stick. Let each student pick a Chinese vegetable from the book, draw a picture of it on one side of his poster board, and label it with its Chinese characters. On the top portion of the other side of the poster board, write the name and pronunciation of the vegetable along with a description. Students may wish to research their vegetable further with encyclopedias, the Internet, etc. Glue the craft sticks to the garden signs. Display the garden signs by sticking them into a sheet of plastic foam covered with brown tissue paper. If desired, let students design vegetables from paper and other craft materials to add to the display after a few days, as if the vegetables had grown in the garden.

EXPLORING POND LIFE

Introduce students to this self-sustaining but fragile habitat that provides food and shelter for a diverse population of plants and animals… the pond!

Did You Know?

- Most animals that swim in a pond, like beavers, muskrats, and frogs have special clear eyelids that protect their eyes when swimming underwater.
- Ponds are important rest areas for migrating birds, providing shelter and food during long flights.
- Pond scum, or algae, produces a large portion of the oxygen in a pond, but can kill the life in a pond if it grows out of control.

Literature Selections

Around the Pond by Ann C. Cooper: Roberts Rinehart Publishing, 1998. (Informational book, 48 pg.) Full of information about different animals that live in a pond habitat.

Around the Pond: Who's Been Here? by Lindsay Barrett George: Greenwillow Books, 1996. (Picture book, 48 pg.) A brother and sister walk around a pond, picking blueberries and discovering clues to the animals that have visited the pond.

Pond Year by Kathryn Lasky: Candlewick Press, 1997. (Picture book, 32 pg.) Two little girls explore the pond near their house throughout the year, enjoying the changes and new surprises each season brings.

What's in the Pond by Anne Hunter: Houghton Mifflin Co., 1999 (Informational book, 32 pg.) A small format book with two pages devoted to each of the ten pond animals featured. Nice up-close illustrations of each animal.

Paper Pond

Turn a corner of your room into an inviting pond habitat. Cut a pond shape from blue butcher paper and tape it to the floor. Cut tall grasses and reeds from green paper and tape them to the walls around the "pond." Add plants and animals to the pond as students complete the crafts in this chapter. Place a basket of pond-related literature beside the pond along with "rocks" (pillows) and "moss" (carpets) for comfortable seating. Play an audio tape of crickets or outdoor sounds and let students enjoy the beauty of your class pond while reading about fascinating creatures.

Pond vs. Lake

Dive into the facts that differentiate ponds and lakes. Post green butcher paper on a wall or board and glue on two large pond shapes. Write *pond* or *lake* above each. Ask students to write facts about lakes and ponds in the appropriate place. During your study of this chapter, let students add to the pond list, including animals and plants found there.

Pond
fresh water
shallow
still water
rooted plants in middle
fills and dries up easily
light can reach bottom
can freeze solid

Lake
salt water or fresh
deep
can have waves
rooted plants only at edges
does not fill or dry up easily
light does not reach bottom
does not freeze solid

The Story of a Pond's Life

"It was a dark and stormy night . . ." Ponds, quite often, do begin this way. Tell the story of a pond's life cycle (see story below). Have students draw the following at the appropriate times: a side view of a hole in the ground, color the hole blue, add plants and animals, color the hole brown, then add trees.

A strong wind uprooted an old tree and left a large hole in the ground. Heavy rains and the flooding of a nearby river caused the hole to fill with water. Breezes carried cattail seeds to the new pond where they sprouted. Ducks came to play in the water and brought algae, fish eggs, and duckweed in their feathers. These plants and animals grew and other animals like beavers, dragonflies, and frogs came to the pond. Eventually decaying material started building up at the bottom of the pond until the pond had filled in and dried up. This new soil was rich with organic materials which caused many new plants and trees to grow there. Eventually, a forest replaced the pond.

Pond Dioramas

"To everything, there is a season" is especially true of ponds. A pond looks very different from season to season as the plant and animal life changes. Students can show these changes with dioramas. Divide the class into four groups, one for each season. Give each group a box with the top and one long side cut out, and let them decorate it using paper, paint, and other materials. The inside of the box represents underwater and the outside is the area around the pond. Stretch plastic wrap across the top of the box for water (a piece of plastic foam could be used for ice in winter). For example, the fall group could decorate the outside of their box with a muskrat lodge, brown topped cattails, and fall leaves resting on the surface of the water. The inside could show lilies and duckweed on the bottom, and frogs and turtles preparing for winter by burying themselves in the mud. After each group has completed its box, display the boxes and let each group present its pond to the class.

63

Cattails

Children will see that cattails are aptly named when they make these fuzzy fall versions from felt, paper, and cotton.

1. Place cotton balls along the edge of a sheet of 9" x 12" brown paper and roll it up around the cotton. Tape to secure the roll. Glue dark brown felt around the roll and place a brown pipe cleaner in the top, down into the cotton. **2.** Have an adult use a craft knife to cut a slit in the roll through the felt and paper. Stuff extra cotton balls in the slit so they appear to be coming out of the cattail. **3.** Cut several long leaves from 12" x 18" green construction paper and roll the rest of the paper into a stalk. **4.** Tape to secure and tape the leaves to the stalk. **5.** Push the top of the stalk into the bottom of the cattail and secure by filling in around the stalk with more cotton balls. Prop the cattails around the *Paper Pond* (page 62); secure with tape if necessary.

Cattail Facts

Cattails provide food and shelter for many animals. Red-winged blackbirds nest among the leaves and musk-rats use them for food and nesting material. Cattails are green in the spring, their stalks topped with yellow flowers. In the fall, the soft and brown cattails fill with fluff and seeds. Later, the stalks open and winter winds carry the fluffy-tipped seeds to sprout elsewhere.

Lovely Lilies

Fun is in full bloom when students make paper plate water lilies. To make a lily pad, paint a paper plate green, then cut out a pie-shaped wedge. To make the flower, trace the flower pattern (page 75) onto two paper plates and cut out. Using a pencil, curl the petals of one of the flowers inward and glue on top of the other flower. Cut a strip of yellow paper 2" x 12" and roll around a finger. Tape to secure the roll and cut fringes along the tube. Glue the tube to the center of the flower. Display student lily pads and flowers in the *Paper Pond* (page 62).

Water Lily Facts

The water lily's flat, floating leaves provide shade and shelter for fish and other pond creatures. The leaves have a waxy coating on top so water rolls off and does not build up and sink the leaf. Water lilies appear to be floating freely on the pond, but they really have long stems that reach the bottom of the pond where they are anchored by roots. Water lilies also have flowers that bloom in summer.

Dazzling Dragonflies

What's the buzz about dragonflies? Find out by using tissue paper and pipe cleaners to represent these delicate beauties. Twist a green and a blue pipe cleaner together. Bend over one end, doubling the thickness and flaring out the loop slightly to make a head. Form four thin, white pipe cleaners into wing shapes, thread the ends through twists in the body, and twist to secure. Draw vein patterns on four strips of white tissue paper and glue to the pipe cleaner wings. When dry, trim around the edges. Cut two large eyes from green construction paper and glue to the head. If desired, tie a thread to the dragonfly's body and suspend from the ceiling.

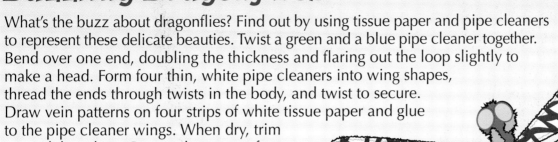

Dragonfly Facts

Dragonflies lay their eggs in the stalks of plants near the water or in the water itself. When the nymphs hatch, they swim and breathe through gills until their wings develop and they leave the water.

Walking on the Water...

is easy if you are a lightweight, long-legged, oily-haired water strider! Demonstrate the part that surface tension plays in this feat by creating water striders from plastic foam. Cut open and flatten a large plastic foam cup and trace the water strider pattern (page 73) onto it. Cut out the water strider and bend down the legs, flattening out the ends of the four longest legs (see illustration). Bend the legs until the water strider is balanced with all legs touching a level surface. Place the water strider into a bowl of water. Note how its light body and long legs (which disperse its weight) are supported by the water. Water striders also have oily hair on their legs that repels water. Observe how the water's surface dips where the legs rest. This is caused by water molecules being attracted to each other and forming what appears to be a plastic film on the surface. Place a penny on the water to show how a heavier, more compact object breaks the surface tension and sinks.

Frogs

Did You Know?

- Many frogs hibernate in the mud at the bottom of the pond, breathing through their skin.

- Frogs catch insects on their long, sticky tongues. They blink as they swallow food whole, using their eyeballs to help force the food down.

- Baby frogs are called tadpoles, polliwogs, or froglets. A group of frogs is called an army.

Literature Selections

Frogs by Gail Gibbons: Holiday House, 1994. (Informational book, 32 pg.) Packed with facts about frogs including their metamorphosis, specialized body parts, and behavior.

From Tadpole to Frog by Wendy Pfeffer: Harper-Collins Publishers, 1994. (Informational book, 32 pg.) Easy-to-read book about the lifecycle of frogs.

Lily Pad Pond by Bianca Lavies: Puffin Books, 1993. (Informational book, 32 pg.) Close-up photos follow the life of a bullfrog.

Frogs vs. Toads

A toad by any other name is not a frog! Frogs and toads are both amphibians and are often confused. Review the characteristics of frogs and toads. Have students write riddles for either amphibian on copies of the frog pattern (page 73). For example, I *have dry, bumpy skin. What am I?* Write the answers on the backs and display the riddles on a bulletin board titled *Frog or Toad?*

Frog
smooth, moist skin
small teeth
narrow body
long back legs
leaps far
lives in or around water
large round eardrums
lays eggs in clumps

Toad
dry, bumpy skin
no teeth
fat body
short back legs
short hops
lives on land
small round eardrums
lays eggs in strings

Life Cycle

Create "It's a Frog's Life" booklets! Have each child fold a 5" x 18" strip of paper into five sections, accordion style. Draw a water line 1/3 from the top and color clouds, water, and water plants. Color and cut out the frog life cycle patterns (page 72) and glue each on a page. Write *egg* and *tadpole* on the first two pages, and *frog* on the last page. As you read the book, explain that a frog begins life in water, breathing through gills and swimming like fish. As lungs and legs develop, gills and tails disappear.

egg tadpole frog

Croaking Frogs

Get students croaking like frogs with this craft that uses a balloon to depict a frog's vocal sac. For the frog's body, have each student cut a paper plate into an oval shape and color green. Cut web-footed, short front legs and long back legs from green construction paper. Accordion fold the back legs and tape the legs onto the frog's body. Paint two egg carton sections green and paint eyes on one side of each; glue in place. Place the short end of a flexible straw into a yellow or green balloon and wrap tape tightly around the mouth of the balloon to seal. Bend the straw at a right angle and tape to the bottom of the plate so the balloon is under the frog's chin and the long part of the straw sticks out along the side. Make the vocal sac expand by blowing into the straw. Have students make croaking sounds as the air escapes from the balloon. Inform students that a male frog vocalizes by drawing air into a special sac under his chin. This sac expands like a balloon and when air is released, it passes over his vocal chords making croaking sounds. Frogs use this sound as a mating call.

Leap Frog

Leap into fun with a paper frog jumping contest! Follow the directions to make an origami frog and then model each step for students as they make their own. Glue on copies of the frog legs pattern (page 73) and green paper eyes. Create a start line with masking tape, push on the top fold to make the frog jump, and measure how far each frog leaps. Then, mask off a finish line and let several students race their frogs. If there are any "short jumpers" in the bunch, explain that they might be toads! Unlike toads, frogs have long, strong back legs that make them great leapers.

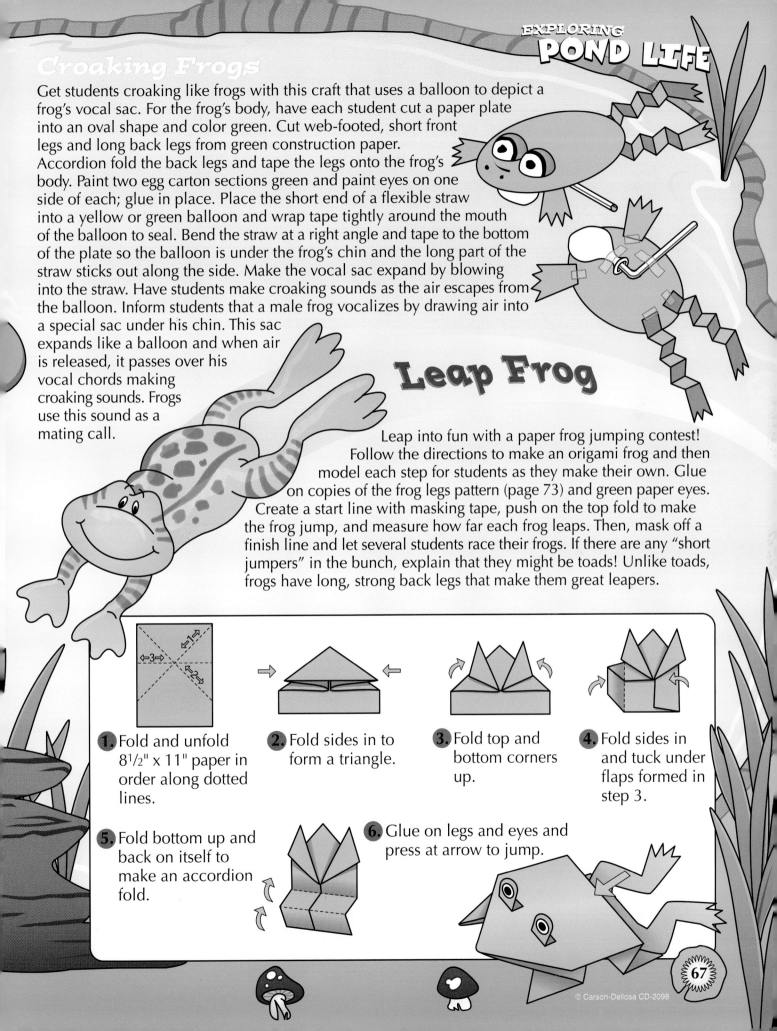

1. Fold and unfold 8½" x 11" paper in order along dotted lines.

2. Fold sides in to form a triangle.

3. Fold top and bottom corners up.

4. Fold sides in and tuck under flaps formed in step 3.

5. Fold bottom up and back on itself to make an accordion fold.

6. Glue on legs and eyes and press at arrow to jump.

67

DUCKS

Did You Know?

- Some ducks are surface-feeders. They dunk their heads, or tip-up, to get food just under the water. Other ducks dive and swim underwater to get food.
- Ducks fly south for the winter in search of open (unfrozen) water in which to find food.
- Baby ducks are called ducklings. A group of ducks is a brace, a flock (in flight), or a paddling (on water).

Literature Selections

All Night Near the Water by Jim Arnosky: Paper Star, 1999. (Picture book, 32 pg.) Beautiful illustrations show a mother mallard duck caring for her ducklings as they discover the sights, sounds, and other animals in the lake at night.

Ducks Don't Get Wet by Augusta Goldin: HarperCollins Children's Books, 1999. (Informational book, 32 pg.) Describes the behavior of a variety of ducks and explains how ducks stay warm and dry in water.

Watching Water Birds by Jim Arnosky: National Geographic Society, 1997 (Informational book, 32 pg.) Realistic paintings accompany informative text for eight unique water birds, including ducks, herons, and geese.

Like Water Off a Duck's Back

How do ducks stay dry when they spend so much time in the water? Their feathers are waterproof. A duck has a gland near its tail that produces oil that the duck spreads over its feathers with its bill in a process called preening. Preening coats the feathers with oil, keeping the water out, since oil and water do not mix. Students can see how preening works by waterproofing their own "feathers." Cut feather shapes from construction paper or fabric. Coat one feather with vegetable oil or shortening and place both feathers on a paper towel. Using a spray bottle, lightly mist water over the feathers and compare the water on the coated and uncoated feathers. Students should notice that the water beads on the coated feather but is absorbed by the uncoated feather.

Duck Feet

Students will like getting their hands on this bird foot experiment! Show how a webbed foot pushes water more efficiently than a regular bird foot by tracing and cutting out duck and bird foot patterns (page 75) from a plastic plate. Drag each through a pan of water, 5-6 inches deep, and compare the amount of water each pushes. By pushing more water with each foot, the duck can move faster without expending more energy. A duck's webbed feet make it awkward for walking on dry land, but helpful for paddling swiftly and gracefully through the water.

Warm as a Duck

Ducks stay warm in cold water because they wear down jackets! Ducks have special feathers close to their skin called *down* that keep them warm by trapping body heat in the air close to the skin. Students can experiment with tissue paper to see how air trapped next to a duck's body keeps in heat. Have one child hold a sheet of tissue paper over the hand of a partner. Ask the partner to breathe through the tissue and feel the heat on her hand. Then, let two more children hold two more layers over the first, spaced about 1" apart so air is trapped between the layers. This time, when the child breathes through the layers of tissue, she should not be able to feel the heat because air between the layers acts as an insulator. Air trapped in down feathers acts like an insulator too, keeping ducks warm.

Colors and Camouflage

These paper fowl will look just ducky on your class pond! Inform students that male ducks are usually brightly colored with extra tufts of feathers or bold patterns to attract mates. The female has drab, mottled colors to provide camouflage at the nest. Provide field guides, encyclopedias, and other references for male and female ducks. Have students choose a male or female duck to paint. Cut out a duck head and neck (see illustration) from an appropriate color. Cut a small triangle for the bill and glue to the head. Fold a paper plate in half for the duck's body and carefully cut a slit in the fold, the same length as the duck's neck is wide. Slide the duck's neck into the slit. Use paint to add color and details. Let students place their ducks around the *Paper Pond* (page 62) and try to camouflage the female ducks.

69

BEAVERS
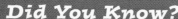

Did You Know?

- Beavers, like ducks, spread oil over their fur to waterproof their coats.
- A beaver can close off its ears and nose and swim underwater for over 15 minutes.
- By damming up rivers and streams, beavers create new pond habitats, providing homes and food for many animals and plants.
- Baby beavers are called kittens. A group of beavers is called a colony.

Literature Selections

Beavers by Helen H. Moore: Mondo Publishing, 1996. (Informational book, 32 pg.) Full of information and illustrations that describe the beaver and its way of life.
Little Beaver and the Echo by Amy MacDonald: Paper Star, 1998. (Picture book, 32 pg.) A beaver hears its echo across a pond. To make friends with the echo, the beaver travels across the pond, meeting friends along the way.

Beaver Buddies

Leave it to students to create paper beavers that show off their most remarkable features—orange teeth and large, flat tails. The orange coating on a beaver's teeth makes them strong. Because its teeth are constantly growing, the beaver must keep gnawing on wood to keep its teeth the right size. A beaver uses its tail to steer when swimming, and to slap the water to warn of danger. Draw fur on a brown paper bag. Draw a face on the bottom of the bag and glue orange paper teeth at the edge of the bag bottom. Make a tail shape on white paper by tracing around the outside of a hand with fingers together, then cut out. Place the paper on a textured surface and rub with the side of a dark brown crayon. Tape the tail to the top edge of the bag. Stand the bag up and place the tail behind to balance it, like a real beaver. Place some beavers around the *Paper Pond* (page 62).

Busy Beavers

Let students work like beavers to build a dam, a lodge (a beaver's home), and a food pile. Place a pile of brown paper and scissors on one side of a room, and cover the bottom half of a bulletin board with blue paper (water) on the other side of the room. Have students "gnaw trees" (cut strips of brown paper) and bring them one by one to the water. To build the dam, glue or staple the paper strips, crisscrossed, in a pile to one end of the board. For the lodge, stack the "sticks" above the water level, then "hollow out" (cover with black paper) an entrance tunnel under the water, and living area at the top of the lodge, above the water level (see illustration.) Lastly, construct a food pile near the lodge. Let students draw beavers swimming, repairing the dam, and in the lodge. Discuss how much work it is for the beaver to cut down trees and build structures in the water. Explain that lodges protect beavers from predators.

TURTLES

Did You Know?

- Turtles are the oldest reptiles still living today and have changed little since the time of dinosaurs.
- All turtles are toothless, but have a sharp beak-like mouth for biting and tearing.
- Baby turtles are called hatchlings. A group of turtles is called a bale.

Literature Selections

Box Turtle at Long Pond by William T. George: Greenwillow Books, 1989. (Picture book, 25 pg.) A nice picture, from the non-swimming box turtle's point of view, of life around a pond.

My Little Book of Painted Turtles by Hope Irvin Marston: Northwood Press, 1996. (Informational book, 36 pg.) Information about the habitat, diet, and hibernation of the painted turtle.

Paint a Painted Turtle

Sunshine on their shells makes them happy! The cold-blooded turtle regulates its body temperature by "basking" or sunning itself on logs and rocks around ponds. The painted turtle is the most common turtle species in North America. They can be found in ponds, streams and wetlands and are typically 4" -10" in size. Enlarge and reduce copies of the turtle pattern (page 74) to make various sizes of turtles, one for each child. Provide green, red, yellow, and brown paint and reference books showing painted turtles and let students paint designs on their turtles. Roll a sheet of large brown construction paper into a tube (like a log) and place at the edge of the *Paper Pond* (page 62). Have students arrange the turtles on and around the log as if basking.

Fact-Filled Turtle

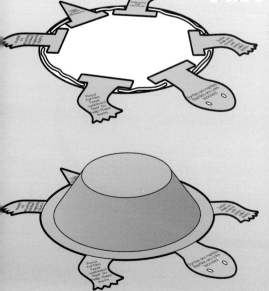

Coax this turtle out of its shell and reveal important turtle facts! Paint the bottom of a small, paper bowl green. When dry, place the bowl upside down on yellow paper. Trace and cut out the circle. Copy the turtle head, legs, and tail patterns (page 74) onto green paper and cut out. Place the turtle patterns around the yellow circle to form a turtle with the tabs well inside the circle (see illustration.) Carefully squeeze glue along the edge of the circle, leaving spaces where the legs, head and tail are placed (see illustration). Place the bowl upside down on the glue and press. When the glue dries, pull the legs, head, and tail out as far as possible. (The tabs should keep them from pulling completely out.) Write facts about turtles, such as, *turtles lay eggs*, or *turtle shells have scales called scutes*, on the turtle's legs, tail, and head. Push them back inside, leaving a small portion sticking out. Be careful not to push them completely inside the shell. To read the turtle facts, gently pull the turtle out of its shell!

71

frog life cycle patterns

intermediate stage 2

intermediate stage 1

tadpole

eggs

adult frog

COPY and CUT

frog

water strider

frog legs

turtle leg

turtle leg

turtle head

turtle tail

copy and CUT

turtle

74

© Carson-Dellosa CD-2098

flower

duck foot

bird foot

Time for FUN & GAMES

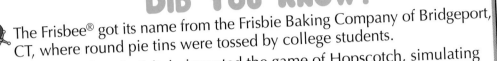

DID YOU KNOW?

- The Frisbee® got its name from the Frisbie Baking Company of Bridgeport, CT, where round pie tins were tossed by college students.
- Roman soldiers in Britain invented the game of Hopscotch, simulating the 400 mile round trip between London and Scotland. Some original hopscotch courts were over 100 feet long, and soldiers often played the game carrying heavy loads of equipment, armor, or supplies.
- In places as diverse as England, Japan, and Africa, people have played Tug-of-War to peacefully settle disagreements.

LITERATURE SELECTIONS

Complete Handbook of Indoor and Outdoor Games and Activities for Young Children by Jean R. Feldman: The Center for Applied Research in Education, 1997. (Game book, 304 pg.) Over 370 games and learning activities.

Outdoor Action Games for Elementary Children by David R. Foster: Prentice Hall, 1994. (Game book, 240 pg.) More than 170 outdoor games and activities emphasize fun and physical fitness for grades K-6.

Reader's Digest Great Big Book of Children's Games by Debra Wise: The Reader's Digest Association, Inc., 1999. (Game book, 320 pg.) Details more than 450 competitive and noncompetitive indoor and outdoor games.

THE GREAT DIVIDE

Assigning teams can be fun and games, too! Use these suggestions when dividing children into groups.

Survey Says Group dog-lovers on one team and cat-lovers on the other. Further divide teams as needed by questioning other preferences: chocolate or vanilla, cake or pie, etc.

Rock, Paper, Scissors Have children form a line to play Rock, Paper, Scissors. "Rock" is shown with a fist, "paper" as a flat hand, and "scissors" with fingers forming a V-shape. Count to three and have students make a symbol. Organize teams according to which symbol they choose.

Jelly Beans Give each student a jelly bean. (Make sure the colors will make even teams.) Students can group themselves according to the color they received and use the candy's color to name their team. For example, *The Orange Tigers*, *The Purple Powerhouse*, etc.

Indoor Games

Rain or shine, these indoor games can become class favorites!

Paper Puzzles

Newspaper puzzles plus teamwork equals the solution to this game! Provide a full-size sheet of newspaper for each team. Cut squares, diamonds, stars, and other shapes from the paper (the same number for each team) and scatter these cutouts around the room. Divide the class into teams of four to six and select a captain for each team. Give captains the sheets with shapes cut out. At a signal, have team members gather the missing cutout pieces and bring them to their captain. Players can use the print on the newspaper to solve the "puzzle." If a piece does not fit, it must be returned to the place it was found. The first team to fit its page back together wins! If desired, laminate the pieces for reusability. For older students, cut out letters to spell a word, use more complicated shapes, or increase the total number of shapes.

Ha! Ha! Ha!

For serious fun, try this game that can be played almost anywhere, any time, and with almost any number of participants (5 to 10 works well). Have players form a closed circle. One player starts the game by saying "Ha!" Play continues around the circle, with consecutive players attempting to add a *Ha!* to the string without smiling, laughing, or making a mistake. For example, the second player would say, "Ha! Ha!" and the third, "Ha! Ha! Ha!," as seriously as possible. A player who fails to remain serious is out of the game, but may now attempt (short of touching or interrupting others) to make the remaining players laugh. The most serious player wins the game by keeping a straight face.

Mystery Word

This double-sided guessing game makes practicing language skills seem like a party! Divide students into groups of six, and choose one player in each group to be *It*. *It* should select a word for the others to guess, and say, "I'm thinking of a word that rhymes with _____." Other students then attempt to guess the mystery word by asking questions which give clues to the word they are guessing. *It* must answer the questions. For example, *It* chooses the mystery word *cat* and says, "I'm thinking of a word that rhymes with fat." The first guesser may ask, "Can I hit a baseball with it?" *It* replies, "No, it's not a bat." If *It* cannot respond with the guesser's word, the guesser reveals his word (*bat*) and gets another chance to discover the mystery word. If *It* is stumped again, the questioner again reveals his answer, but play moves to the next questioner. The first player to guess the mystery word becomes *It* and chooses a mystery word for the next game.

OUTDOOR GAMES

Share these outdoor games with parent volunteers or physical education teachers for special times with your class.

FITNESS FUN

Fitness fun is a hop, skip, and jump away with this team challenge! Compose a list of fitness instructions (see sample at right), and order the same activities differently for each group. Divide the class into four groups and have each choose a leader. At a signal, have team leaders open the directions and lead teammates in performing the activities in the order listed. To emphasize physical fitness, include exercises such as sit ups, push ups, jumping rope, etc. When the activities are complete, reward students with copies of the medal pattern (page 81) to cut out, color, and wear.

SAMPLE FITNESS FUN DIRECTIONS

1. Decide on a team name and tell the teacher.
2. Go to a large area, hold hands, and sing "Ring-Around-the-Rosy" three times.
3. Bunny hop to the nearest tree and give everyone on your team a "high five."
4. Do 10 jumping jacks.
5. Run to the sidewalk, find the chalk, and have each team member trace her hand and write her name next to it.
6. Skip to the blacktop, hook elbows, and jump up and down while singing the alphabet song twice.

CIRCLE-STAR

This team challenge ensures that everyone shares in the fun! Divide students into groups of five and have each group form a circle. Players toss, kick, or roll a ball clockwise to the person two places to their left in the circle. The path of the ball will form a star.

To extend the activity, increase the number of balls being passed around, move players farther apart, or increase the number of participants to create a seven- or nine-pointed star. Have teams compete to see who can first pass the ball around the circle-star five times.

CHAUCER'S CHASERS

Read the children's version of Chaucer's tale, *Chanticleer and the Fox,* (adapted and illustrated by Barbara Cooney: HarperTrophy, 2000) before playing this literary version of Tag! Make bib overalls for the "farmer" by cutting a vest from a grocery bag and adding details with markers. Dress the farmer in the vest and a baseball cap, supply him with small stickers, and have him sit in a chair in a central area. Designate two foxes (chasers) and an area to represent the foxes' den. At a signal, the remaining students—the Chanticleers (roosters) run from the foxes. If desired, design paper rooster and fox tails for students to wear.

When tagged, a player goes to the farmer, who places a sticker on his hand. That player may return to the game. After receiving three stickers, players go to the foxes' den. When the den is full or when only one player remains, the last player becomes the new farmer, and chooses two classmates to be foxes. Stickers are removed and play resumes.

HUMAN TIC-TAC-TOE

Problem solving and cooperation acquire life-size proportions in this version of the classic game! Create a three-by-three grid (large enough for players to stand in) on the ground using chalk or tape. Divide the class into teams X and O, and toss a coin to decide which team starts the game. A player from the winning team chooses and occupies a square, making a giant X or O with her arms. The game continues with teams taking turns placing team members on the squares until one team gets three students in a row, or until all squares are full. If desired, play tic-tac-toe as a trivia challenge or practice test, in which students must correctly answer a question to occupy a square.

OPERATION COOPERATION

Cooperation and problem solving are the goals of this game. Give groups of six players an equal number of carpet squares or pieces of cardboard, and two hula hoops. Mark off starting and goal lines, and explain that the object is to get the entire team to the goal following these rules:

1. Players' feet can touch the ground only inside hoops or on top of squares. If a player steps off a square or outside a hoop, that team starts over.
2. As many people as can fit on a square or in a hoop at one time may do so.
3. Players may move or reuse hoops and squares.

When all teams have crossed the finish line, discuss the benefits of teamwork and problem solving, and reward each player with a Terrific Teamwork! award (page 81). Increase the challenge by providing fewer materials or increasing the distance to the goal.

BARNYARD

With a cluck-cluck here, and a moo-moo there, Old MacDonald would feel right at home in this searching game. Hide small objects of one type around the playing area. For example, plastic Easter eggs, wrapped candies, or other small treats. Divide players into equal teams of three or more and tell them what they are searching for. Have each team select a leader, a home base, and a barnyard animal to imitate. One group may elect to be cows based in a pasture. Pigs, sheep, or ducks could have styes, pens, or ponds. At a signal, players (except leaders, who stay at the base) search for the hidden objects, which only leaders may collect. A player summons her leader by imitating her barnyard animal: clucking, quacking, mooing, etc. The leader runs to collect the object before another leader can retrieve it. Leaders may carry only one object at a time back to home base. When all objects have been retrieved or after an allotted amount of time, the team with the most objects wins. If edible objects are used, let players enjoy them as a snack.

79

THE OLYMPIC GAMES

Every two years, athletes from around the globe gather to compete for gold, glory, and greatness. Find out more about the most famous games in history!

DID YOU KNOW?

○ The first games were held in Greece in 776 B.C. with one event, a foot race called the *stadion*. Other events were added over time, including longer foot races, chariot and horse racing, boxing, and the Pentathlon—a five-part contest which involved throwing the discus, throwing the javelin, jumping, running, and wrestling.

○ The colors of the Olympic rings (blue, yellow, black, green, and red) were chosen because at least one of these colors can be found in the flag of every nation.

SCHOOLYMPICS

Bring home the gold with your school's own Olympics! Here's how:

GET READY!

Olympic Teams Divide students into teams representing different countries. If possible, encourage other classes to participate. Teams can design their own flags and compose team songs.

Olympic Events As a class, vote on which events to complete. Track and field events, such as running, jumping, and throwing, work well. Consider sprint races, relay races, three-legged races, sack races, and standing and running jumps. Other fun activities are the "shot put," a softball throw, or beanbag toss. A Frisbee® makes the perfect modern discus—have your Olympians throw for distance or accuracy.

GET SET!

Staying on Track Enlist volunteers—administrators, teachers, parents, even students—to act as judges, referees, timekeepers, etc. Students involved in this process can feel ownership of the games!

In Training If possible, allow students to "train" during recess for several days or weeks. Have students use stop watches, yardsticks, etc., to keep track of time or distance. Graph the students' progress and keep in a notebook or display on a bulletin board.

Go!

Off to a Good Start Stage opening ceremonies for your games, including a parade and torch ceremony. Have students dress in the colors of their team and march as a group around the class, gym, or playground. Make an Olympic flame from colored tissue paper attached to a large cardboard tube.

A Great Finish After the games, celebrate with a medal ceremony! Copy the medal pattern (page 81) and have students color and cut out their medals. Collect the medals to present at a ceremony. For Olympic-style awards, punch holes in the ends of a medal and use yarn, string, or ribbon to form a necklace.

Terrific Teamwork!

Name _____ Signed _____ Date _____

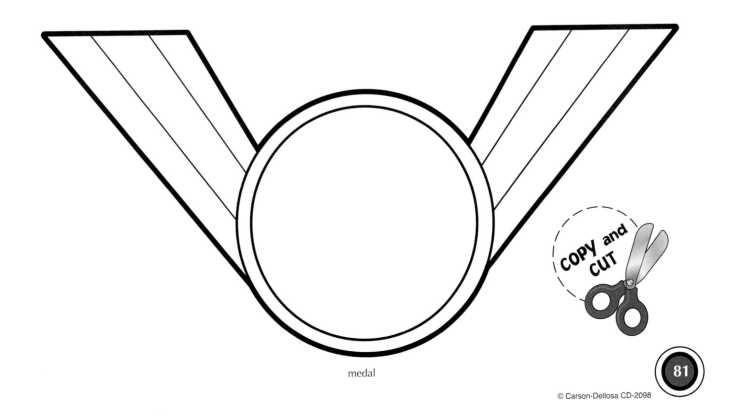

COPY and CUT

medal

STAR GAZING

People have been looking towards the heavens for thousands of years to establish calendars, navigate ships, and satisfy curiosity about the universe. Help students satisfy their curiosity about the stars and celebrate Astronomy Day. (This day is observed in April or May on the Saturday that occurs closest to the first-quarter moon.)

DID YOU KNOW?

⭐ Looking at the stars is like traveling back in time. Since it takes a long time for light to reach Earth from outer space, when we look at a far away star, like Deneb in the constellation Cygnus (Swan), we see it as it was 1,630 years ago!

⭐ Although there are billions of stars in the universe, on a clear night only about 2,000 stars can be seen with the naked eye.

⭐ People who live in the southern hemisphere can see stars that people in the northern hemisphere never see and vice-versa.

LITERATURE SELECTIONS

Stargazers by Gail Gibbons: Holiday House, 1992. (Informational book, 32 pg.) A complete and easy-to-understand explanation of stars, constellations, telescopes, and stargazing.

Starry Messenger by Peter Sis: Farrar Straus & Giroux, 1996. (Informational book, 40 pg.) A simple biography of Galileo with Caldecott honored illustrations and some of Galileo's own notations.

Stars by Seymour Simon: Mulberry Books, 1989. (Informational book, 32 pg.) Stunning photographs accompany the science behind stars, their lifetimes, galaxies, nebulae, etc.

SPACE AND TIME

Early humans plotted the movement of heavenly objects and created calendar systems based on their observations. Ancient Greeks built on these ideas, Galileo built on the Greeks' ideas, and so on, ever advancing our knowledge of outer space. Isaac Newton noted this progressive history of astronomy when he said, "If I have seen further than others, it was because I stood upon the shoulders of giants." Have students research these "giants" of astronomy. Give each child the name of a famous astronomer or astronomical device to research, such as Copernicus, Hubble, or Stonehenge. Have students write short reports on large star shapes, then display the shapes in chronological order on a wall, showing the expanding knowledge of the universe.

Nicolaus Copernicus was born in 1473. He studied medicine and law, but he really liked astronomy. He was one of the first people to think the Earth revolved around the sun.

Johannes Kepler was a German astronomer who was born in 1571. He proved that the orbit of Mars is an ellipse. He believed that the universe was beautiful.

82

TAKE A CLOSER LOOK

Gaze at the stars through a homemade telescope, like Galileo. In 1609, Galileo was the first person to look at objects in space through a telescope. He discovered mountains on the moon, individual stars in the Milky Way, and moons around Jupiter. Make telescope viewers that show the *constellations*, or star groups, and let students guess their correct names. Give each child a long cardboard tube and have her trace the circles at the ends on black paper and cut out. Place one constellation pattern (page 86) over a circle and use a straight pin to poke holes through each dot on the pattern. Use a hole punch to make a viewing hole in the center of the other circle. Glue each circle to an end of the tube. Cover the tube with aluminum foil and tape to secure. Cut two small strips of black construction paper and tape them around the center of the tube. To view the constellation, close one eye and look through the viewing hole while pointing the telescope at a light. Let students take turns looking through each others' telescopes and guessing the constellations.

SIZING IT UP

Why do the moon and the sun appear to be about the same size in the sky, when the sun is almost 400 times larger than the moon? The key is that the sun is 93 million miles away from Earth and the moon is only 240,000 miles away. Distance is also why stars much larger than our sun appear to be so small. Show students how distance affects the apparent size of an object. Give small groups of students each a small ball (1" diameter) and a large ball (3" diameter). Place the balls side by side on the edge of a table. Kneel on the floor so that your eyes are at the same level as the table top. Close one eye and look at the balls. At the same distance from your eye, one appears larger than the other. Have one student slowly move the large ball along the table, straight back from the viewer until the balls appear to be the same size. (The distance should be about 30".) Add different sized balls and let students measure and compare the distances at which balls appear the same size.

DISAPPEARING STARS

Abracadabra! Make the stars appear and disappear before students' eyes with this simple experiment! Purchase glow-in-the-dark stars and arrange them on the ceiling or wall. Completely black out the light from any windows by covering them with dark paper. Leave the lights on all day to "charge" the stars. Tell students that the lights in the classroom represent the sun's bright light. Then, turn off the lights to simulate nighttime. The stars should be more visible when the "sun" is turned off. Turn on the lights again to simulate daytime and have students compare the visibility of the stars. Explain that the stars are not visible during the day because of the brighter light from the sun.

83

STAR STUDDED STORIES

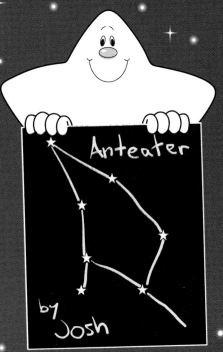

The ancient Greeks and people in all parts of the world have seen pictures in groups of stars and made up stories about them. The Big Dipper has been described as a bear, the leg of an ox, and a drinking gourd. Give each child a sheet of black construction paper and a handful of foil star stickers. Let him place several stickers around the page at random and exchange papers with a classmate. The paper he receives will be his constellation. Using a piece of white chalk, have him play dot-to-dot with the stars, creating a shape for the constellation. After he decides what the shape looks like, he could name his constellation and write a story about it. Display the constellations on a bulletin board or bind them in a traveling book and send home for parents to see.

SHOOTING STAR FACTS

When you wish upon a shooting star, you are not wishing on a star at all. Let students make shimmering shooting star pictures and learn what they really are—bits of dust, chips off asteroids, and other bits of metallic rock called *meteors* that enter Earth's atmosphere and burn up. Some meteors are no bigger than a grain of sand, others are larger and may not burn up completely in the atmosphere. Regular meteor showers are seen at the same times and in the same areas of the sky each year. (Refer to the chart below to learn about common meteor showers.) Give each student a 12" x 5" strip of black construction paper and a 12" x 14" piece of dark blue construction paper. Have each child draw the silhouette of a skyline on the black strip and cut it out. Then, glue the black silhouette to the blue paper, lining up the bottom edges. Cut small yellow paper squares and glue them on the silhouette to look like lighted windows. Draw stars with glue, spaced out on the sky, and sprinkle with gold or silver glitter. Using yellow or white colored pencils, let students write facts about meteors trailing from each star.

Shower Name and Location	Date of Maximum Shower Activity	Hourly Rate of Maximum Shower Activity
Quadrantid (Draco)	January 3	10-50
Lyrid (Lyra)	April 21	5-15
Eta Aquarid (Aquarius)	May 4	10-20
South Delta Aquarid (Aquarius)	July 27-29	10-20
Perseid (Perseus)	August 12	30-70
Orionid (Orion)	October 20	10-30
Leonid (Leo)	November 17	10-20
Geminid (Gemini)	December 13	30-80

COMET BOOKLETS

No giggling allowed with these comet books! Have students create booklets about comets which include the definition of a comet, the parts of a comet, what happens to comets as they orbit the sun, (see illustration) and the names of famous comets, such as Hale Bopp, Halley's, Ikeya-Seki, Shoemaker-Levy, and Hyakutake. Often referred to as dirty snowballs, comets are large balls of frozen gases and dust that orbit the sun. As a comet approaches the sun, it starts to melt and dust and gas are released. This dust and gas trails behind the comet in a bright display. As comets pass the sun, their tails are forced to point away from the sun because of the pressure of the sun's radiation.

coma

nucleus

tail

Comets orbit the sun. Their comas and tails develop as they get close to the sun. A comet's tail always points away from the sun.

STAR GAZER

When ancient Greeks looked at the night sky, they connected the stars and gave them names based on pictures they saw. We still use these star groups, or constellations, to help identify and locate stars. Let each student make his own star chart to learn the names and locations of common stars and constellations. Have each child cut out the star chart pattern (page 87) and a 8" black construction paper circle. Let students trace over 4-5 constellations they know with colored pencil to help them stand out (Orion, Big Dipper, etc.). Place the star chart cutout (page 86) about 1" from the edge of the black circle and trace. Cut out the traced shape and tape a piece of clear plastic (laminating scraps work well) over the hole on the back of the circle. Write the cardinal directions, as shown on the last illustration below, around the cut-out area. Line up the star chart pattern under the circle and place a brad through the center at the North Star Polaris. (Because Polaris is roughly above the North Pole, as the Earth rotates, the other stars appear to rotate around Polaris.) Students can turn the wheel to see how the sky changes through the year. Line up the following stars or constellations with the "N" to show the sky during each season: Winter–Draco's head, Summer–the star Capella in Auriga, Spring–Cassiopeia, Fall–the Big Dipper.

AMY'S STAR FINDER

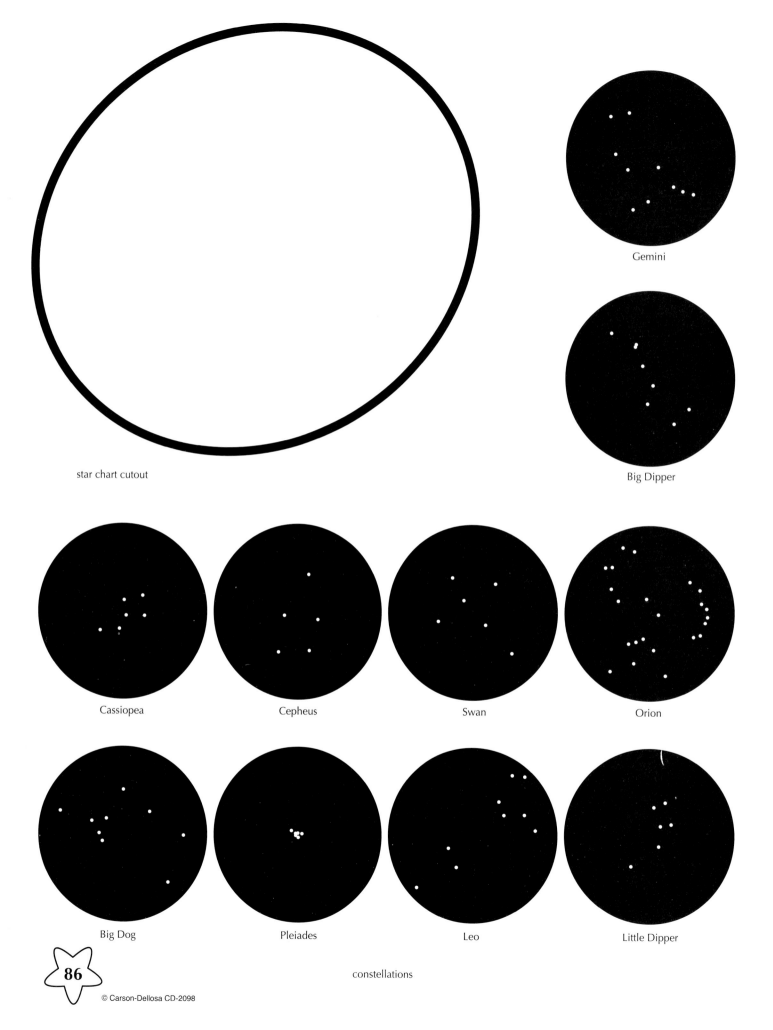

star chart cutout

Gemini

Big Dipper

Cassiopea

Cepheus

Swan

Orion

Big Dog

Pleiades

Leo

Little Dipper

constellations

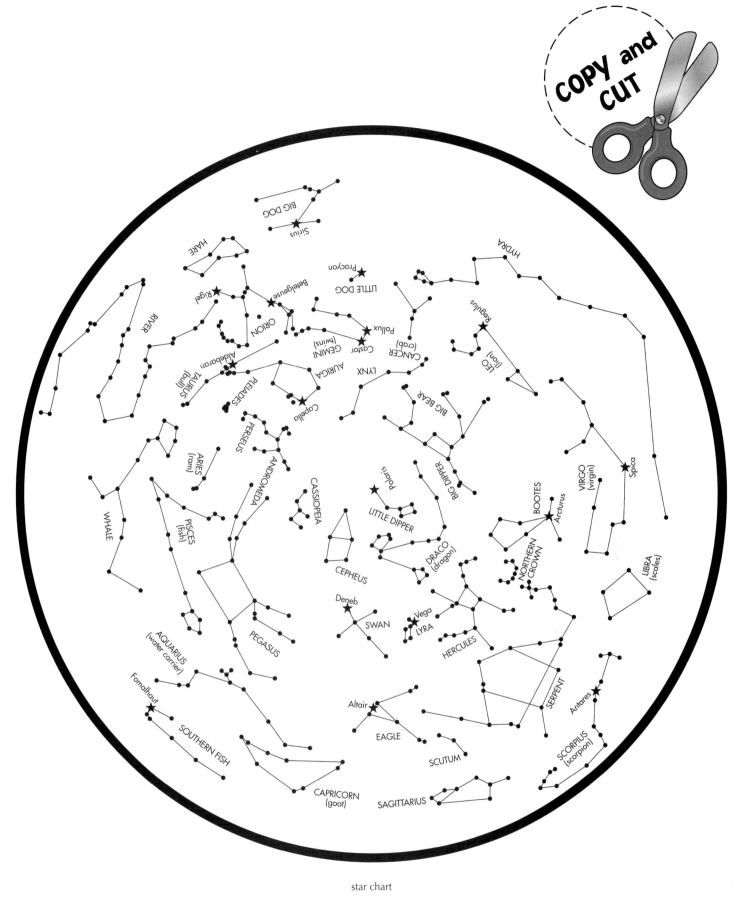

BIG DOG
Sirius
HARE
Procyon
LITTLE DOG
HYDRA
RIVER
Rigel
Betelgeuse
ORION
Pollux
Regulus
Aldebaran
GEMINI
(twins)
Castor
CANCER
(crab)
LEO
(lion)
TAURUS
(bull)
AURIGA
LYNX
PLEIADES
Capella
BIG BEAR
ARIES
(ram)
PERSEUS
BIG DIPPER
Spica
ANDROMEDA
VIRGO
(virgin)
CASSIOPEIA
Polaris
BOOTES
Arcturus
WHALE
LITTLE DIPPER
PISCES
(fish)
NORTHERN
CROWN
DRACO
(dragon)
LIBRA
(scales)
CEPHEUS
Deneb
SWAN
Vega
LYRA
AQUARIUS
(water carrier)
PEGASUS
HERCULES
SERPENT
Fomalhaut
Altair
Antares
SOUTHERN FISH
EAGLE
SCORPIUS
(scorpion)
SCUTUM
CAPRICORN
(goat)
SAGITTARIUS

star chart

★ = brightest star in the constellation

• = stars

87

Celebrate the Family

Family Month is celebrated Mother's Day through Father's Day each year and is dedicated to encouraging the appreciation of families and children. Relate Family Month to students with these activities and top off the celebration with a Family Night at school!

Did You Know?

★ In many Asian countries, people put their family names before their first names.
★ The Zaramo tribe, who live in Tanzania, are matrilineal. Lines of descent and family names are passed through women.

Literature Selections

A Chair for My Mother by Vera B. Williams: HarperCollins Children's Book Group, 1985. (Picture book, 32 pg.) A girl and her family save their money to buy a new chair.
Families are Different by Nina Pellegrini: Holiday House, Inc., 1991. (Picture book, 32 pg.) An adopted Korean girl finds that there are many different types of families.
Fathers, Mothers, Sisters, Brothers: A Collection of Family Poems by Mary A. Hoberman: Penguin Putnam Books for Young Readers, 1993. (Poetry, 32 pg.) Thirty poems about family life.
Like Jake and Me by Mavis Jukes: Alfred A. Books for Young Readers, 1987. (Picture book, 32 pg.) Alex thinks he and his stepfather have nothing in common.
The Relatives Came by Cynthia Rylant: Aladdin Paperbacks, 1993. (Picture book, 32 pg.) Relatives from another state come to visit.

This is my mom. She is smart and she likes to read. She reads at least one book a week!

Faux Family Photos

Get to know students' families by compiling fun "photo" albums. Give each student several sheets of construction paper to fold in half to make albums. Then, provide several white construction paper squares, crayons, and small black construction paper triangles. Instruct students to draw one family member on each white square and then glue a "photo" to each page of her album. Have children glue triangles in each corner so the picture looks like a photo displayed in an album; then write a few sentences describing each family member. Punch three holes on the left side of each album and provide ribbon or yarn to thread through the holes. Display the family photo albums in a basket for students to share.

That's My Family!

Piece together family pride with collages! Provide construction paper shapes, such as squares, circles, rectangles, etc. Have each student use the geometric shapes to construct each member of her immediate family and glue them to a piece of construction paper. Then, let students cut out words from magazines and newspapers that describe their families (let younger students cut out pictures) and glue them on the construction paper figures. Provide markers for students to decorate their collages and to write their family names across the tops of their papers. Display the family collages on a bulletin board or wall. For Family Night (pages 90-91), place each collage on the appropriate student's desk.

Family Message Center

Families will get the message with this handy message board. Have students bring in favorite family photos or draw their families on construction paper. Glue the pictures to the top of an 8½" x 11" piece of poster board. Let each student decorate around the edges of her poster board with sequins, glitter, etc., and write a family slogan at the top such as *Together We Stand*, or *Loving Each Other*, etc. Cover the poster board with contact paper and glue a magnetic strip to the back. Punch a hole in the corner, thread yarn through, and tie an erasable marker to the end. Let students take their message boards home to put on their refrigerators so family members can write messages to each other.

Who's Home?

Keep family members guessing with this game! Let each student cut out a copy of the house pattern (page 92). Then, have students trace another house on construction paper and cut one window or door on the house for each member of their immediate family. Glue the construction paper house on top of the paper house, making sure not to glue down the door and window flaps. Attach the roof with a staple in the top corner. Draw a picture of a family member under each flap and write clues about that person's identity on the flap. On Family Night (pages 90-91), let students challenge their family members to guess who is in each area of the house.

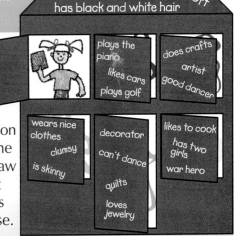

Family Night Fun

Celebrate families at school with the following Family Night activities. If Family Night is not possible, have one or more family members visit class or let families prepare audio or video tapes or scrapbooks for students to bring to class.

Family Night Invitations

Plan for Family Night by having students make invitations on decorated copies of the house pattern (page 92). Decide as a class when the Family Night celebration should take place and at what time. Let each student write the information on the house and give it to her family. Students can invite parents, siblings, and grandparents to Family Night. Include a place on the invitation for the number of family members attending so you will know how many to expect. Students should return the completed invitations to class.

You're Invited to Family Night!

Wed. May 14
7:00 pm

How many attending?

Meet, Greet, and Eat!

Help families feel at home during Family Night. Create a home setting in the classroom by putting down rugs, providing pillows to sit on, and using lamps for lighting. You may also wish to cut out a TV shape with a welcome message and hang it on a wall, frame classwork and artwork and hang it in a picture gallery style on walls and bulletin boards, push desks together to create activity centers, and arrange chairs in conversation groupings. Set up a table with plates and napkins and ask each family to bring their family's favorite snack to share. While everyone enjoys the food, allow students to present their families with *Faux Family Photos, That's My Family!, Family Message Center,* and *Who's Home?* crafts (pages 88-89). Take pictures during the party to create a Family Fun Night bulletin board display. Or, place the photographs in an album and display with the *Faux Family Photos* (page 88).

Family Scavenger Hunt

Get families to mingle with this social scavenger hunt. Before Family Night, make a list of things that might describe a family, such as *likes movies, goes camping together, has all boys, has a pizza night,* etc. On Family Night, give each family a list and instruct them to find a family that fits each category. Challenge players to find a different family for each category. Set a timer for 15 minutes and then see which family has the most categories completed. Award the winning family with a special prize, such as a bag of jelly beans or a gift certificate to a family restaurant.

FAMILY PENNANTS

Show off family pride with these informative family pennants. At a center, provide several construction paper triangles in different colors, ribbon, tape, markers, crayons, glitter, etc. Have each family member decorate a triangle according to his hobbies, interests, characteristics, etc. Then, let families decorate a triangle with the family name. Connect the triangles with colorful ribbon, placing the family name in the center. If desired, have each family present its family pennant to the group. Hang the pennants around the room and encourage families to take them home at the end of the evening.

Tracking Traditions

Send families on a mission of tradition! Set up a table and provide construction paper and crayons. Tell families that they will collectively make a book called *A Big Book of Family Traditions*. Have each family draw a picture of themselves engaged in a family tradition (holidays, everyday events, etc.) and then write about the tradition below the picture. After Family Night, bind the pages into a book and let each student take the book home for an evening to share with his family.

Picture This!

Create instant smiles with this family photo craft. Set up a station in the classroom with poster board, cloth scraps, sequins, buttons, etc. At the station, take an instant photo of each family. Then, let each family use the craft materials to create a decorative frame for their portrait. Have families glue the frames to their photos and keep them as mementos of Family Night.

Robert, Henry, Judith, & Jamie Davis

COPY and CUT

house

May Day

Every year on the first of May, people gather for music, dancing, pageants, and flower-filled festivities. Traditionally, May Day is a time for hope and joy, celebrating new life, community, and the coming of spring. The May Day holiday dates back to Floralia (Flor•ALL•ya), an ancient festival honoring Flora, the Roman goddess of spring. Parades of singers and dancers carried statues of Flora past a flowering tree, a predecessor of the Maypole. As time passed, participants began choosing a May Queen and sometimes, a May King, to preside over their celebrations. In 16th century England, people called these figureheads Maid Marion and Robin Hood. In present day England, children gather flowers and travel from house to house, exchanging the flowers for coins. Children then toss the coins into wishing wells or give them to charity.

Maypole Merriment

Welcome spring with May Day dancing! The Maypole is the most widely recognized symbol of May Day celebrations in England. Traditionally, a pole made from the trunk of a tall birch tree was decorated with wildflowers. Construct a class Maypole by attaching a dowel rod or wrapping paper tube to a cardboard base on the ground. Decorate the pole and top it with real flowers or student-decorated copies of flower patterns (page 44). Usually, dancers wearing bells and colorful costumes danced in and out around the pole, weaving colorful ribbons around it. When the dancers changed directions, the ribbon unwound and got longer, symbolizing the lengthening of days in spring. Attach streamers to the top of the class maypole and have students "braid" the steamers around the pole while dancing. If desired, play a game in which students try to unwind the streamers without letting go of the ends.

Gorgeous Garlands

Fun will blossom when making May Day Garlands! Garlands are traditionally made to wear or use in May Day dances. They are made by winding greenery, flowers, and ribbons together to form wreaths of different sizes. To create garlands, have students cut out pictures of flowers from magazines and glue them on rings of green construction paper. For a 3-dimensional alternative, make a garland base using a wooden ring or wire coat hanger twisted into a circle. Wrap greenery and flowers, attached with colorful string, around the garland base. If greenery is not available, cut green plastic wrap, trash bags, or tissue paper into strips and crinkle them for texture. Secure the greenery with string. During May Day, competitions are held to choose the prettiest or best-made garlands. If desired, have a class competition and display the garlands on a bulletin board.

May Day (continued)

Flora and Jack

In Roman mythology, Flora was the goddess of flowers and springtime. Festivals in her honor included parties, plays, and pageants. Flora was depicted as a beautiful maiden wearing a crown of flowers in her hair, surrounded by garlands. Another figure associated closely with nature in England is Jack-in-the-Green, a symbol of man and nature. Jack-in-the-Green, also called the Green Man, is surrounded by (and sometimes made up of) plants and flowers. People often dress up as Jack and walk in May Day parades. Describe Flora and Jack and have students brainstorm words that remind them of springtime and nature. Have them use these lists as reference for drawing Flora (springtime) or Jack-in-the-Green (nature).

FLORA

Jack-in-the-Green

May, Beautiful May Poems

One May Day tradition says that washing in the morning dew on May Day will keep a person young and beautiful (see illustration at right). Talk about flowers blooming, trees budding, birds singing, and other things that represent spring. Have students write poems about the beauty of springtime and the first day of May. Have each student decorate a paper with a thumb print flower border on which to write a final copy of her poem. Display the spring poems on a bulletin board.

The fair maid who, the first of May,
Goes to the field at break of day,
And washes in the dew from the hawthorn tree,
Will ever after handsome be.

May Day Dancing

Dancing is an important part of the May Day celebration in England. Morris Dancers (Morris is a style of May Day Dance), Square dancers, and ribbon dancers can often be seen in parades accompanying Jack-in-the-Green or dancing near the Maypole. Ask groups of 5-6 students to create their own dances. Explain that Morris dancers carry garlands and perform energetic dances, tapping wooden sticks and waving large handkerchiefs. If you have bells, rhythm sticks, or other musical instruments, distribute to students. If desired, allow students to integrate props such as ribbons, garlands, or streamers into their dances. Finally, have the groups perform their dances, explaining the meaning of their colors and dance movements. You may also have groups choose an idea or emotion to portray through their dances and let classmates guess what the dance expresses.

Kodomono-hi
(Children's Day)

In Japan, May 5 is called Kodomono-hi (ko•do•mo•no•hee), or Children's Day. It is a day set aside to celebrate the health and happiness of children and to promote strength of character. Children's Day is celebrated by flying kites, pinwheels, and streamers, and enjoying special holiday foods and drinks.

Character Kites

Good character will be up, up, and away with this activity. To remind children that they can be successful if they work hard, each member of a family flies a colorful, tube-shaped carp kite called a *koinobori* (KOY•no•BOR•ee). These kites are flown from pinwheel-topped bamboo poles on rooftops or in gardens. Make carp character kites and discuss good character. Tell students that in Japanese culture, the carp, or *koi*, is a symbol of strength, determination, and success.

Give each student a paper lunch bag to decorate like a fish. Make the open end the fish's mouth and the folded side the tail. Have each student list positive character traits and things people can do to be successful, and write them on the carp's scales. Decorate the kite with glitter, ribbons, buttons, etc. Thread yarn through the corners of the fish's "mouth," add streamers, and display the character kites in your classroom. If desired, talk about character traits associated with other animals, such as wise owls, loyal dogs, noble lions, and proud eagles.

Free Wheeling

Blow some fun students' way with these pinwheels! Let each student make a pinwheel like those flown with the Koinobori kites by drawing and cutting out a 5" square of paper. Use a ruler to draw lines connecting opposite corners of the square. In the center of the square, make a small circle by tracing a nickel or button. Carefully cut to, but not through, the center circle. Pull every other corner in to the far end of the circle. Do not crease. Secure the pinwheel corners to an unsharpened pencil by pushing a pin or thumbtack through the four folded corners, the center circle of the pinwheel, and through the pencil eraser. Attach ribbons and streamers and display the pinwheels along with the *Character Kites* (above). The streamers are called *fuki-nagashi* (FOO•kee•na•GA•shee) and symbolize freedom.

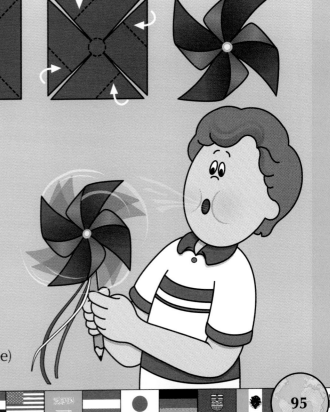

Cinco de Mayo

Cinco de Mayo, Spanish for the fifth of May, is more than just a holiday. It is a reminder of a time when common men fought for freedom with uncommon bravery. In 1862, Mexico was very poor. When Mexico's President, Benito Juarez, said that Mexico could not afford to pay back money it owed, France's Emperor Napoleon III sent a powerful army to take control of Mexico. On May 5, 1862, Mexican general Ignacio Zaragoza led his army of poor peasants and farmers into battle against the French at the city of Puebla. In a heroic display of courage and patriotism, the outnumbered Mexican army forced the French fighters to retreat. General Zaragoza became a national hero and Cinco de Mayo became a day for people to celebrate pride, patriotism, and the bravery of those who fought against the odds.

Maraca Music

Today, people both in Mexico and the U.S. celebrate Cinco de Mayo with parades, mariachi music, folk dancing, feasting, and fireworks. To celebrate, let students make their own maracas. Have each student decorate a short cardboard tube with colorful designs, sequins, and buttons. Then, close off one end of the tube with wax paper or plastic wrap and rubber bands. Put a handful of dried beans inside the tube, then close off the other end in the same way. Explain that people dance traditional Mexican folk dances like *La Cucaracha* to festive music played by mariachi bands. Traditional instruments include maracas, violins, guitars, trumpets, accordions, and bass guitars. Celebrants often sing loudly and accent their songs with shouts of "Yi-yi-yiii!" Play Mexican music and let students use their maracas.

South of the Border Snacks

Treat your maraca musicians to one or both of these quick and easy Mexican snacks.

Sweet Cinnamon Snacks

Fry flour tortillas lightly in oil and then sprinkle with sugar and cinnamon. Cut into wedges and serve.

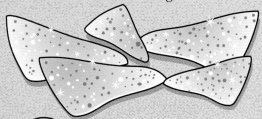

Tasty Tacos

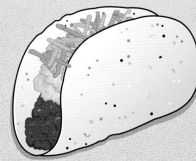

1 lb. ground beef
Taco seasoning mix
12 taco shells
Shredded lettuce and cheese
Taco sauce

Brown ground beef and drain. Add taco seasoning mix according to package directions. Heat taco shells in oven for 4 or 5 minutes until shells are crisp. Fill heated shells with meat and top with remaining ingredients. Makes 12 tacos.

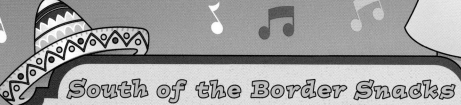